# How To Train A Puppy:

A Step By Step Guide to Raising Your Dog In Just 7 Days: Basics, Commands, Tricks, Skills, Exercises And Everything You Need So Your Pup Will Understand You!

## Adam Bennett

*To my wife Cecilia*

*for always listening to me*

*supporting me*

*and encouraging me.*

*If it wasn't for you, I'd be lost.*

# Table of Contents

## Do you enjoy listening?

If you love listening to audiobooks on-the-go or enjoy narration as you read along, I have great news for you.

You can download the audio book version for FREE just by signing up for a FREE 30-day audible trial!

Check out my *How to Train a Puppy* audiobook.

# Introduction

Greetings readers! Congratulations on taking the first step of your journey! The first time you bring a puppy into your home, chances are that you will have as much fun and will encounter as many surprises as real parents do. Suddenly you have a little whirlwind in your house that takes hearts by storm, turns everything upside down and gets ideas you never even dreamt of. Yes, a puppy knows how to charm people.

Nevertheless, puppies need proper training right from the start. The human world is huge, exciting and often dangerous for animals. Puppies must learn at an early stage to adapt to this environment. This includes: Following commands, fitting in with the human family, understanding what is forbidden, getting used to a leash and even coping with being alone. Remember that every puppy becomes a full-grown dog after some time. The saying "You can't teach an old dog new tricks" does have some truth to it.

Especially during the first weeks of their lives, puppies go through important phases that shape them for their entire future. Those who are too careless or too harsh now or those who miss important moments in their puppies' life and make other training mistakes will find it very difficult to get rid of these flaws and mistakes later on.

Love, consistency, and knowledge are the key factors for successful puppy training. There are also numerous questions you should ask yourself before buying a puppy - first of all: Which dog suits my circumstances? Which breed is less suitable for me? What do I have to have in my home for the dog, what do I have to protect?

In this guide, you will learn everything you have to know to have a smooth start with your little four-legged friend. How you can teach him obedience and how he internalizes the most important commands early on and at the same time you will learn to understand your puppy and how you should respond to him in certain situations.

*Adam Bennett*

# Chapter 1    Puppy    Training    For Beginners

Puppy training can start as soon as your dog enters his new home. In fact, the way you receive the puppy is already a training-starting period, allowing you to set the tone to what is about to come.

If you've known dogs, then you know that these fellas are professional jumpers and chewers. Their commitment to chewing your sofa will break your resolve to save it. And so you also know that this training will require love, time and commitment but most of all it will require patience. Patience comes from being prepared, something you can trust this book to help you with. The first thing you need to know is that puppies are just like babies, which is why they are shockingly absorbent of everything we introduce them to. Although, the important thing to note is that the success and strength of your training process and relationship respectively is the 'way' in which you tell your puppy to sit.

Dogs are sensitive and empathetic creatures; taking an overbearing approach to train them is never a good idea. As a matter of fact it appears to be quite the mistake when people reassess their training times with their dogs. Only because in the olden times, the rather cack-handed approach was the way to go, one need not follow it because in order to build an empathetic and loving relationship, it is important to step back from conventional knowledge at times.

These so called age old, time tested conventional or traditional training methods involve the use of binding and captivity to instill discipline, the overt use of leashes. These young puppies have the energy and excitement of a human teenager gone on rebellion and they do not like being on a leash. Apart from being inhumane and cruel, the part that imparts redundancy to these methods is that such puppy training is mostly inefficient. There is a two pointer explanation to this - most dogs do not realize the purpose of a leash and neither do they realize the strength of it due to which the whole process can become a painful confusion for these puppies. Another point being the rather fragile necks of these puppies which can twist with the excessive pulling.

Now going positive is sure a U turn from the convention but it indeed is one of the best ways that can ensure that the puppy too feels loved and cared for throughout this crucial training period. Positive reinforcement as is clear from the name talks about reinforcing a certain positive nature - in this case it is done by giving rewards for showing positive behaviors. It reworks the puppy's brain into a more understanding and receptive one.

Well if you are still not convinced then you must know Bo! The Obamas' dog, Bo, has been trained using the same methods by some of the best trainers. It has as a practice become extremely popular due to its effectiveness.

The concept note of positive reinforcement is far from complicated. It is something you can also see in human behavior. The chances of an action increases if it is associated with a reward. The brain automatically processes things so fast for that momentary reward that there is no space for anxiousness or misunderstanding. All this jazz but still the best part of this exercise is that you can begin your puppy's training the day you bring that bundle of joy home. The crucial thing to note here is that you reward this good behavior with treats or cuddles if you do so immediately after the dog performs the action. This is the only way that the tiny puppy brain will make a direct correlation between a reward and its preceding action. It is indeed obvious that the more you pet and praise your pup, the better he/she will learn what action gets them treats and what doesn't.

The Benefits

Many training methods do not involve training from the very start, well because they have certain rather negative processes which can scar young puppies. This makes positive reinforcement, one of the only viable, successful and empathetic training concepts that dog owners can practice if they have young pups. It is effective in establishing certain basic rules in much less time. When it comes to a dog owner in this over demanding and fast world; time is the primary concern and although this process is extremely fast and effective - the best quality of this pathway is that it forges a fun and engaged relationship between dog and owner.

Training for Everyone

A really important benefit of this process is that it involves the entire environment and family of the dog rather than them having only one master. This makes sure that all family members are involved in forging a caring and loving relationship with the pup. Such a holistic method weeds out the many chances of training going wrong. For example, a child playfully pulling the leash on a young pup can prove harmful for both of them; teaching the kid to use these doggy treats in their own way would forge a more understanding relationship. Dogs already love kids, and then they would just go gaga over them.

Communication Establishment

This technique is the only way to establish a thriving language and communication between you and your pet. You have to use a certain form of command when you tell your puppy what it is that they need to do and once that is done, you can throw a treat in the air and expect a big happy grab. As it is in the nature of dogs to please, they will start repeating their good actions to get nothing but more praise from you. This allows the communication to happen in a rather clear way.

Now let us try and understand a bit about how punishing actually does not work primarily because the communication is unclear. Now imagine if this new family member pees all over your exotic carpet. Your reaction would be anger, and you would not think much before smacking a rolled up magazine to teach him/her what is off limits. Now here, research indicates that the chances of your puppy not understanding what the smack is for are pretty high. For example, they can just associate this act of punishment with not urinating in the presence of a person which is also indicative from the fact that many dog owners which use traditional training methods find their dogs making a mess in their absence. This confusion also somewhere is speculated to arise from the fact that your dog just does not expect you to lash out on them and hence communication with fear as a medium is definitely not clear.

On the other hand, where there are rewards and praise, the puppy always seems to find a direct correlation which encourages it to repeat the desired behavior. To do is easier than to not do.

Perfect for All Breeds

Different breeds, different behaviors. There is nothing new in it, in fact it is only common sense when you see the difference between a Labrador or a Doberman! This leads us to the fact that all training methods cannot be suitable for all kinds of dogs. The dangers are widespread - using punishments on already aggressive dogs can make them harsher and aggressive in turn. Or if it is a fearful dog, they might just become more fearful and reduce interaction, become depressed and also might not respond to alternate behavior correction measures.

A need comes to find something so fundamental with respect to dogs that the difference of practice that arises due to breed becomes a null value. In simple words - positive reinforcement is something all breeds of pups can be trained for. No matter the kind of dog, the kind of trauma associated, positive reinforcement is a no harm procedure.

Bond Strengthening

The bond between the dog owner or adopting family and this new member is the primary reason why you are even adopting a pup in the first place. It is a sensitive bond and needs to be handled with care. Choosing such a way of instilling order that is through positive reinforcement is a full proof way to ensure a healthy, loving and beautiful relationship, where the bond grows deeper with each passing day. This is a huge difference from the rather traditional forms of training.

Somewhat the basic task of this training is to make you unknowingly look at things from the perspective of the puppy. This is important as what you expect from this puppy is to look at things a bit from your perspective and not pee on that exotic couch as much as it might be his/her favorite task to do. Since you expect a less involved mammal to understand you, you as a more evolved being are completely capable of doing this task through the techniques of positive reinforcement.

Mental Stimulation

Boredom in humans, can make them question the meaning of everything. So in a similar manner, boredom in a puppy's life can lead to some serious behavioral issues. If your puppy has not been playing and is just laying in a restricted space for a long time it will try and let you know that it is bored by excessive scratching, digging or chewing. Initially by having these training sessions with the puppy you can increase their general excitement and also make them burn some essential energy.

It's Fun!

It is essential that if a long commitment with respect to puppy training is to be maintained; it MUST be fun! The idea is to keep training positive, short, direct and upbeat in spirit. You'll be surprised by how much fun it is for you. Shortly after you start these minor trainings - the puppy would look at these activities as playtime which will only support your training process. Teaching new disciplines would be as cool as a breeze for both of you.

The Rewards

The primary object of positive reinforcement is nothing but the reward itself. As explained earlier in order to instill some order or command in your puppy, all you need is to reward them at a correct and immediate time in order to let them know what they are getting rewarded for. Over the time they will learn the pattern and repeat in order to earn more treats.

The certain few criticisms of positive reinforcement methods have come from seeing the rewards as bribes. The rebuttal to that lies in the very different natures of bribing and rewarding. When you think of your pay check at the end of the month, do you even for a second feel that you have been bribed into working? Because that is not the case, in this case you have worked very hard for a certain period of time for which you have been given your due share. If you were not paid at work, or given other psychological, social and economical benefits, you would have been so unmotivated that you would stop going to work. The same goes for the puppy - it is doing these actions in order to live in houses, which is not their most natural habitat - they put in the extra work and these good puppies deserve their due shares (treats!).

Also a treat does not only have to be something that can be eaten. In that way, the dog would only respond nicely when it is hungry but rather these treats need to be versatile and dependent on your particular dog and its habits and likes. Knowing the puppy is quite important to finding the key to their motivations.

Treats

It is for a reason, that treats have been deemed as the most common and obvious reward. Thanks to their ease of dispensability and the fact that they are really immediate rewards. Also puppies are hungry most of the time and super interested in eating in they're growing years. This eagerness of the reward makes them learn much earlier than many other old dogs. A doggy treat is a great choice for a reward.

But also as we discussed earlier, boredom is as real for animals as humans so it is important that there should be other rewards. Other reasons being -logistically one could be out of treats, or the puppies might just not be able to digest properly.

Games

Treats can fill the stomach, make a dog really happy but the other thing that gets them going is playing games with humans. You could also spend some time in order to figure out what kind of games your pup is interested in. Not all pups are great at fetching. Some might simply like a good tug of war. Once figured out, give them commands and reward with swiftly throwing a ball out to the yard.

Attention

Almost all dogs like attention but some of them just simply need it more than others. But if it is the case that your dog is more attention savvy, use it to your advantage. You could use this attention and hustle as a reward to whenever they perform a desired action. For example, if your dog wants some serious petting, make them go through a few previously taught commands and on successful attempts, give them enough attention which could be pats, snuggles or belly rubs! In the case that the puppy fails to do the action, the best strategy is to step aside for 20-30 seconds only to return and try again. Such an activity will make your pup realize that completing an activity leads to hugs and snuggles.

Going Outdoors

Allowing your puppy to run in the fields is a rather unconventional method of training the dog. Especially when it comes to dumping habits. For instance, you could put a leash on the pup and let the pup take you to its dumping ground, do not allow him/her to explore much but rather just wait until the pup relieves itself. If it does not urinate, the best thing is to go inside and try again in a while. The time when the puppy does relieve itself, the positive thing to do would be to take them for a treat worthy walk with lots of exploring. It will then associate the smell of the excretory spot as an opportunity to score a reward.

The training sessions explained within the book will use puppy treats as our go to reward as they always seem to do the trick a bit faster than other things. Once again before we delve deeper, any kind of innovative reward could be used for a suitable puppy but it is extremely important that the reward is delivered immediately after the action or the entire exercise could be very confusing for your puppy.

# Chapter 2    Tips    and    Information Before Training Your Puppy

Training your dog can make you feel overwhelmed; it doesn't matter if you are focusing on basic training, such as sitting and lying down, or advanced techniques, such as dog sports. There are moments you will become frustrated, no matter how patient and calm you feel. Then, there are those wonderful moments—the times your dog succeeds at a new trick. It's these moments where you feel that all your hard work has paid off.

But why do people focus on the end result when they are training? Professional trainers will tell you that you have to celebrate every moment your dog made an effort with their training, even if they made a mistake.

Celebrating the missteps your dog takes during training won't make them put in less effort. It won't tell them that this moment is "good enough." It will tell them that you are proud of them for trying. You're proud of them for working hard and you want to reward them with positive reinforcement. Doing this will get your dog focused on the task and want to make you happy again.

Celebrating the moments with positive reinforcement, even when a mistake is made, is one of the first points you need to understand when it comes to training.

## What to Know Before Training

Celebrating is not the only point you need to understand before you start training. You need to understand that your dog's personality depends on how well they will train. You need to know about training tools, how your dog's age matters, and how your mindset matters.

## Put Thought Into the Name

Naturally, you will choose a name that you love, but if you know you'll spend a lot of time training your new family member, it's important to think of a name that will catch your dog's attention. Names with strong consonants that are short work great. They will perk up your dog's ears, making it easier for you to catch their attention. Some great names to consider are Ginger, Jack, and Jasper.

You may think you can only give your little eight-week-old puppy a name and not your older dog you received from the shelter. It's important to know the name of your dog from the shelter tends to be temporary. While this isn't always the case, most shelters don't know the dog's name when they receive them. Call your dog by their shelter name and notice their reaction. If they don't respond, they don't know that you are calling them, and you can rename your dog. Even if you have a dog that responds to a name, you can still change it. This can give you a good start on learning how to train your dog.

## Have One Consistent Way to Grab Your Dog's Attention

Dogs are easily distracted by their environment, especially puppies. This causes problems with training because their owners feel they aren't listening to them. In reality, your dog became distracted and didn't know you were talking to them. By setting up a way to grab your dog's attention, such as calling their name, you will train them to look at you.

For example, you notice your dog is in the yard sniffing something on the ground, but they are too close to the road. Because the way you get your dog's attention is to snap your fingers, you head outside and snap your fingers twice. Even though you are several feet from your dog, they are used to this sound and know you are calling to them. They look up and listen to your command to "come."

## Consistency Is Key

One of the strongest ways to effectively train your dog is remaining consistent. It is always possible you won't catch your dog in action or be unable to reach your dog when they misbehave, meaning you have to let this one slide as they won't understand what they did wrong. When it comes to these moments, you need to realize they happen. The trick is to not let them happen often. Professional trainers say you have about five seconds to correct your dog's behavior. Once this time passes, you need to let it go and try to catch them in the act the next time.

## Patience Is Another Key

Another strong key feature when it comes to training is patience. If you have expectations that your dog will learn to sit by the end of the day, you must lower your expectations. It will take days to weeks to train your dog one trick and you will never stop training.

You will need more patience for a dog you just brought home as it takes them time to adjust to their new environment and for an older dog. Senior dogs are slower than puppies. They aren't going to catch on to new tricks as quickly and can show more stubbornness because they are used to their ways. However, with patience, consistency, and positive reinforcement you will teach your old dog new tricks.

## Prepare for Your Dog to Come Home

Just as people prepare to bring their baby home, you want to prepare to bring your dog home. This doesn't mean you need to set up a whole room, but make a spot for their bed, crate, food, water, and some toys. Your dog needs their space just like you need your space. It'll help them feel more at ease and comfortable in their new environment. Plus, they will immediately start to feel that you care.

You hear about dogs sleeping in bed with their companions, but this isn't the idea you want to give a dog you're training. Teach them everyone sleeps in their own space. If possible, give your dog space that isn't around other people or pets. It's common for people with more than one dog to set up their kennels or beds right next to each other. If your dog's laying next to each other brings comfort to them, it's fine to allow it. But, make sure that both your dogs understand they each have a bed and space. There will be times they want to be alone.

Other ways to prepare for your dog to come home:

- **Plan the arrival**: If you work during the day, try to bring your dog home on a Friday night or Saturday morning. Spend the weekend getting to know your dog by taking them around their new environment, observing their behavior, and playing with them. Give them as much love and support as possible because they are frightened and uneasy about their new home. They need to trust you before they can truly enjoy their new surroundings.

- **Gather any supplies you will need:** At first you may think your dog needs a couple of dishes for water and food, a bed, crate, and a few toys. However, there are a lot of other supplies you can bring into your dog's environment immediately to help them prepare for training from the start. For example, a leash, collar, and any other training tools you will choose. Also, a couple of old towels or rugs are a good idea for several reasons. It can give your dog's space a more comfortable look and be quickly available in case your dog has any accidents. Even a potty-trained dog can have accidents when they first come to a new house.

- **Think about your other pets:** Animals are sensitive, and they will get jealous of the new family member if you don't give them enough attention. It's common to tell ourselves our other pets "will adjust" and we "don't need to worry." The truth is, you should worry about how all your pets feel. Try to play with all of your pets, make sure you give everyone equal attention, and talk to them when they walk by. Animals love to hear your voice and it makes them feel comfortable.

- **Make sure everyone is healthy:** Even if you are told the shelter gave your dog a check-up, bring them into the veterinarian's office as soon as possible. Not only can you ensure your dog is healthy, but your vet and dog can start their friendship. You should also take your other pets in for a check-up, especially if it's been a few months or more. It's always a good idea to make sure everyone is healthy for the new arrival. Unless you are going to breed, think spaying or neutering your dog if they aren't already. The veterinarian will guide you through this process.

## Don't Push Aside the Crate

It's easy for you to see a crate as a jail cell for a dog, but dogs see a crate as a place to call their own. As long as you don't make your dog stay in the crate most of the day, you will find your dog lounging in their crate at times.

One factor to consider with a crate is how you will use it. If you want to use the crate as a way to punish your dog for bad behavior, you won't want them sleeping in the crate. In this case, you will want to think about getting a bed and a crate or two different types of crates. You don't want to tell your dog to go to bed in the same crate you give them a time out in because they can confuse the two meanings. If your dog feels you are angry with them during the night, they aren't going to sleep well, causing them to become sick or depressed.

## Think About Your Training and Discipline

Some people use training as a way to combat disciplining their dog. They believe training their dog to listen to their commands and using a firm voice is all they need. For most dogs, this will work as long as you are training your dog correctly and consistently. Even if this is the way you want to go, it is helpful to look into the best ways to use any form of discipline. You also need to be aware that certain forms of discipline will have serious consequences.

Correctly disciplining your dog is not an easy task. It will take planning and ensuring that every family member is on the same page. This is something you will also need to do with training. To effectively discipline your dog, consider the following tips:

- Your dog shouldn't know that you are disciplining them. If your dog realizes it is you, they will misbehave when you aren't around. This is one reason why a lot of people turn to training in order to teach their dog how to behave.

- Your dog lives in the moment. If you discipline your dog a minute after the unwanted behavior, they will associate the discipline with their current action and not their previous action.

- Do not use discipline with an aggressive dog. This can make their aggression worse. If you find yourself struggling with an aggressive dog, it's time to think about obedience classes or a professional trainer who can help you.

- You need to teach your dog a wanted behavior to replace the unwanted behavior. This is another reason people like to use training. However, you should never think of training as a form of discipline.

- Don't severely discipline your dog for a small crime and don't weakly discipline them for a big crime. This is a difficult imaginary line to find, but it is necessary. Think of it this way: If you are too harsh on your dog, you're going to make them frightened and weaken any trust and respect within your relationship. If your discipline is weak, it won't cause the dog to work on changing their behavior.

There are many ways that you should never discipline your dog because it will cause problems in the future.

- You should never hit your dog, not even a pat on the nose. Dogs are highly sensitive animals and this action will cause them to trauma, especially if it happens continuously.

- Never knee or kick your dog. You can easily hurt them, and it will cause them trauma.

- Don't "rub your dog's nose in it." If your dog has an accident, look over your training procedure or take your dog to the veterinarian to ensure it's not a medical issue.

- Don't yell at your dog. This is often our automatic reaction when they run into the street or do something that's unsafe. Yelling is similar to hitting or kicking with a dog, as it can easily traumatize them.

- Don't jerk the leash when your dog pulls you on a walk. Take time to train your dog so they don't take part in this behavior.

## Common Dog Training Methods

There are many methods you can use to train your dog. In fact, you may find yourself overwhelmed by all the methods and struggle finding the best one for you and your dog. You might find yourself using one method, but not liking it after a while because you don't feel like your dog is responding to the method. While it is likely your dog needs a different method, it's important that you analyze your training method before changing on your dog.

There is a lot of disagreement with the various methods I discuss in this section. For example, many people won't use the e-collar because they think the shock will harm their dog. While it can, if you use the e-collar correctly your dog will barely notice the shock and still respond by stopping the behavior.

## Positive Reinforcement Training

You always want to give your dog positive reinforcement when they do something well. Therefore, this type of training should be a part of any other form of training. However, it can also stand alone. This type of training has been around for a long period of time, but it's gained popularity over the last few years.

When you focus on positive reinforcement training, you are constantly giving your dog rave reviews when they show good behavior. The main idea behind this training method is that dogs will naturally repeat behavior when they receive positive reinforcement. As long as you remain consistent with the positive reinforcement, your dog will follow the behavior that gives them the attention they desire.

When a dog exhibits unwanted behavior, you simply don't respond. You don't talk to them, you don't pet them, and you don't give them any type of positive reinforcement. This is one of the biggest problems people have when using positive reinforcement. They don't understand how you can ignore your dog's bad behavior and it will go away.

It is important to note that the more stubborn breeds will have a harder time learning through this method because they are more likely to continue their negative behavior. While they love positive reinforcement as much as an easily trainable dog breed, they won't care that you are ignoring certain behavior. Instead, they will see this as an open window to continue the behavior. Dogs that are easily trainable and more sensitive will notice you don't pay attention when they perform certain actions and more than likely stop the behavior or at least decrease it.

Using positive reinforcement training means you have to be on your toes with your dog at all times. You will need to supervise them well to give them positive reinforcement within seconds of their good behavior. If you don't catch them soon enough, they won't understand why they are receiving the extra attention from you and will associate it with the behavior they exhibited at the time.

When you start rewarding behavior for training, you will give them positive reinforcement every time they exhibit the behavior. After they catch on to the training and their behavior becomes more regular and natural, you will start giving them positive reinforcement every other time, then every third time, etc. You want to gradually decrease the positive reinforcement you give with that behavior. This is another piece people struggle with during positive reinforcement training. People want to give their dog attention all the time, but they can't when using this form of training.

## E-collar Training

The e-collar is known as the electrical collar and delivers signals, such as a tone, vibration, and shock to your dog's neck. It's important to realize the e-collar is not meant to be a way to discipline your dog. Unfortunately, there are people who use their e-collar for this purpose. They will give their dog a shock every time they do something wrong. The e-collar is meant to be a teaching tool, one that trains your dog to stop the unwanted behavior without realizing it is you giving them the shock. Instead, they believe their behavior caused the shock, making them stop the behavior over a period of time.

There are various types of e-collars and you need to choose the one that is right for your dog. For example, if you are training your dog to hunt, you will purchase a hunting e-collar. For focusing on house training, you will purchase a yard e-collar. You need to look at the basics of the e-collar because each one is a bit different. For instance, a yard e-collar ranges to ½ to ¾ of a mile. This means you can send signals to your dog with the remote until they pass this point. The furthest e-collars tend to go is about a mile. These are typically the e-collars used for hunting.

If you choose to use the e-collar, you want your dog to become used to the device before you start using it. It is advised that you let your dog wear it for a week before you turn it on and start training. You want to train during this time as the e-collar is not necessary for early training. When you start using the e-collar, set it on its lowest stimulation level. If your dog reacts by turning their neck a bit, they can feel the shock and you shouldn't increase the stimulation level. Most dogs will feel the shock at the lowest setting.

Do not use e-collars on dogs younger than five to six months old. While some smaller e-collars will fit on them, most people feel the training is still in its early stages where it is best to use verbal cues and hand gestures to train your dog.

# Chapter 3    5 Basic Rules of House Training

Now that we have had some time to look at the benefits of crate training your puppy and some of the steps that you need to take to make this happen, it is time to take a look at the basics of house training your puppy. For many new dog owners, house training is going to be seen as one of the hardest parts of raising a puppy. However, if you are consistent and do it in the right manner, you will find that a lot of the time commitment and the frustration will be gone. And this is where we are going to start ourselves off with this chapter.

Before we dive in, though, remember that your puppy is going to be an individual, and they will respond to the training at their own pace. There are tips and tricks that you can use that will make the practice a bit easier, but for the most part, each dog is going to respond at their own pace. Don't be persuaded by the marketing pitches of training programs that say how your puppy has to be trained in six days or less. Sure, there are some puppies that can learn quickly, but most will take a bit more time.

What we mean here is that you should not come to this step with a timeline or expectations that are unrealistic. Understanding that your puppy is going to be unique in the manner that they can respond to the training is going to put you at ease and will give you the right mindset to actually get through the house training without a lot of frustration along the way.

The first question that a lot of people have when it comes to house training their puppy is when they should get started. The best option here is to be prepared to begin some kind of house training the moment that you bring the puppy home. Follow these guidelines in order to train your puppy in the fastest way possible and minimize the number of accidents your puppy has in your home.

The first step that you take is to show your puppy the area that is designated for the potty, and this is where you will need to place the puppy each time that you take them outside. The puppy will obviously not go potty in the exact spot each time, but taking them over to this spot when you bring them outside will make a difference. Eventually, the puppy will catch on that this is the spot they need to use to go potty if you do it enough times.

The amount of time that your puppy is going to be able to wait before they have to go outside and go potty will vary based on their age. If you have just brought home an eight week old puppy, then being consistent and taking them out to go potty on a regular basis is going to be the best bet. This is going to be the way that you teach them where and when to go potty faster than before. In fact, one of the best ways that you do this is to take them out to go potty every twenty minutes when they are not in their crate.

Now, there may be times when you bring home a puppy that has been with their past caregiver for some time. It is easy to assume that you don't need to take the puppy outside as often when they are older, especially when they were doing well with their previous home. Of course, you need to remember that when the dog comes home with you, they are in a brand new environment, and they are pretty much starting things over. You may not want to go every twenty minutes when the puppy is older and house trained, but do not go over an hour when they are outside of the crate until they adjust to the new place.

This may seem like a lot of times to take the puppy out, but the more that you do it, the quicker they are going to learn about this process, and the quicker they are going to get house trained. The shorter the amount of time between the breaks to go potty, the faster the house training will go. This results in a puppy that learns the rules of the home faster and will help you to have fewer accidents.

Another tip that you may want to work with while training your puppy is to always bring some treats outside during the potty break. This way, when the puppy does go potty outside, especially when they do it in the designated area like you show them, they can get praise and a reward all at the same time, reinforcing what you are trying to teach them.

The next question that a lot of people are going to have when they work on house training their puppy is what they should be doing when they take the puppy outside. Remember that the routine that you set up is going to be the most effective method to use to reduce the time it takes to train the puppy. When you establish a consistent routine that is associated back with an activity, it is going to start ingraining itself as a habit in the cognitive processes of the brain.

The routine does not have to be super complicated in order to work for your needs. A good routine that can help you to speed up the house training process between you and your puppy could include something like the following:

1.  When it is time, you can take your puppy outside to the designated area for going potty.
2.  Tell them the command of "go potty."
3.  Once the puppy does go potty, give them a treat to let them know that they did something good when they were able to go potty outside. Make sure to give the puppy treats or some physical affection and a lot of praise when they do decide to go potty outside.

It can be as simple as that. In addition to following the steps above for house training, crate training can go hand in hand with house training, and they can work to make the process work better for both of them. One of the keys, in fact, of this is that each time you take the puppy out from the crate, take them right outside to go to the bathroom. If they end up having some accidents in the time they walk from the crate to the door, then you may need to carry the puppy outside so that you don't end up with this kind of issue.

Now, you need to make sure that you are not letting the puppy stay in the crate too long when you are potty training. Most puppies are going to have an instinct to keep their area or their den clean. This isn't going to happen around the house because they can just go and walk away from it. But when you keep them in the crate, they do not want to dirty up the area around them. You can use this to your advantage to work on potty training because the puppy is going to be less likely to have any accidents in the crate.

The problem is that you could be tempted to leave the puppy inside the crate for too long. The puppy has a small bladder, and they are not going to be able to hold it in for 8 hours or more at a time. If you do end up needing to leave the puppy in for longer, then you need to make sure that you or someone else stops by and lets them out once or twice during the day. This helps the puppy to get some relief and will reinforce what you are trying to do with your house training.

You may also run into the issue of the puppy taking a long time to go potty when you take them outside. The first thing to remember here is that you need to be patient. Sometimes the puppy gets distracted and wants to look around and explore the world around them. This causes them to not go potty the second that you take them out, even if they have been stuck in the crate for a long time period before this.

You may find that you need to wait for about 15 minutes or so. The more time that you give the puppy to go potty in the beginning, the faster they will go potty once outside, and the faster you can get the house training done. This may seem like it is going to take forever, and you may be impatient, but just think of how much faster it will make the whole house training process. In the beginning, these 15 minutes may need to be expanded out to 30 minutes or more for the best results.

If you take the puppy outside and wait 15 to 20 minutes and they don't go potty, bring them back inside. Put them back into the crate for a bit, maybe ten to fifteen minutes, and then take them back outside. Repeat this until the puppy does go potty outside, and then give them a big treat and a lot of praise for doing a good job.

This can be hard, and it is going to take a lot of your time in order to see the results. But this is the best way for you to get the house training done. It is also crucial that you actually make your way outside with the puppy and watch them go puppy. This allows you to tell if you are actually getting the puppy to go when they are outside. Over time, the puppy will get the process down, and you will be able to give them the freedom to go back outside and inside any time that you would like.

Of course, if you have a young puppy, there are times when an accident is going to happen inside during play time or the few times that you keep the puppy out of the crate. As the owner, you need to watch how you react to the accident that the puppy is having. This is going to make a difference in how successfully the house training process is going to be.

It is important that you move quickly during this time. running is the best. Whenever a puppy is about to go in the house, sprint over to them and see if you are able to catch them before they even start. Even if the puppy is already going potty, get to them as quickly as possible and still pick them up. The puppy will stop going as soon as you pick them up, so don't hesitate here and then take them out to their potty spot as quickly as possible.

Now, there have been a lot of false options that have been given on what to do when your puppy goes potty inside. These things are going to reinforce a negative behavior at best and can make the puppy aggressive in the worst. Some of the things that you need to make sure that you never do when you see your puppy going potty inside include:

1.  Scold the puppy for an accident that you did not personally see them do.
2.  Just watch your puppy when they have this accident without doing anything to put a stop to it.
3.  Yell or be really aggressive in the manner that you use to scold the puppy.
4.  Put your puppy into the crate as a form of punishment for having the accident. Remember, the crate is not supposed to be a form of punishment for your puppy.
5.  Rub the nose of the puppy in this accident.

Out of these myths, the first one about scolding your puppy for an accident that you didn't actually see being done is the most common mistakes that dog owners will make. They won't even remember that they went to the bathroom in the house, and this scolding is not going to benefit either of you. Yes, it is unfortunate that they did this, but at this point, you need to just clean it up and move on, working to prevent it the next time that it happens.

Being able to debunk some of the myths about house training your puppy is so important to this guidebook. Often we think what we are doing while training the puppy is for the best, and it ends up undermining all of the good things that we try to do. Even if you have made some of these mistakes in the past, though, you can follow the tips in this chapter and in the whole guidebook to make sure that you avoid this problem and get the best results with house training your new puppy.

# Chapter 4    Housebreaking

There are two main ways to housebreak your new puppy: paper training and crate training. Crate training is one of the quickest ways to housebreak your pup but not the best method if you must leave your pup for a longer period of time than your pup is able to hold it. For people who must work all day or be away for long periods of time, I recommend a combination of both methods.

## Paper Training

The paper-training method is where you use newspapers and encourage your puppy to use these for going to the bathroom. You can also use special 'wee wee' pads that are scented with a chemical that attracts the puppy to use them. You can get these at any local pet store. They can make training easier but they can be more costly as well. If you intend to continue using the pads, make sure you start with them and not paper. Don't mix newspaper and pads or your results will be very inconsistent.

The first thing you want to do is choose a confinement area, either in a very small room or a room that you can enclose with baby gates. Most people choose a bathroom, laundry room or kitchen area because these rooms are usually covered in tile or other flooring that is easy to keep clean. The confinement area should only be big enough for your pup's bed, food and water bowls, and his designated potty area.

There should be no visible floor space in the confinement area. The floor should have the bed or crate in one section, and newspapers or pads should cover the rest of the space. By using a small area, you are encouraging your pup to use the covered area of the floor to relieve himself. This will get him used to doing his business on the newspapers or pads. He won't potty in his bed or where he eats for reasons we have already discussed, and since it's the only other space available, the potty area becomes a natural choice. The instincts that Mother Nature gave him will guide him away from his 'den' area to eliminate.

When he does soil on the newspapers, try to clean them up as quickly as possible. You may want to consider leaving a rag that has a little of his urine on it in the designated spot to help him recognize where he's supposed to go, if you're using newspaper. The pads are already scented to attract the puppy to go there. There are also house-training sprays you can buy at any big pet store that serve the same purpose. The pheromones in them attract puppy back to the right spot. These sprays can also be used outdoors if you want to direct him to a certain area.

Once your pup becomes accustomed to pottying on the newspapers, you can make the covered area smaller. You should have noticed which section of the area he has used most often, and keep all that section well covered. Start uncovering the area very close to his crate/bed and bowls. The goal is to continuously limit the designated 'inside potty area' by making the papered area smaller and smaller at the same time giving him frequent access to his 'outdoor potty area'. Therefore it's important that you spend as much time as possible with your puppy so you can get him to his outdoor area as often as possible.

The key to quick and successful housebreaking when using the paper training method really depends on how much supervised training you spend with your pup. The more times you can get him outside to do his business and reward him, the quicker he will learn.

## Crate Training

The second method of housebreaking involves the use of a crate. You want to make sure the crate isn't too large—it should be just big enough to fit a sprawled sleeping puppy. As discussed earlier, dogs do not like to urinate or defecate in their sleeping areas or dens. Once pups are safely mobile, their mothers push them outside so they can go potty.

Crate training helps puppies learn how to control their bladder and bowels. Ideally you should take a puppy outside about every hour to start. Gradually lengthen the time between trips, within the limitations of his little bladder. It's important that you keep your eye on the clock. You don't want to lose track of the time and force your puppy to go in his crate. The more he can feel positive that you'll let him out to relieve himself in a timely fashion, the more incentive he has to wait for you. He wants praise from his pack leader, but he also needs to feel that he can trust you and rely on you.

When your puppy is not crated, watch carefully for signs that he needs to go out. Most dogs have a 'pre-potty' ritual of sniffing, circling, whining, etc., that he'll use to try to let you know what he needs. With a little observation, and a few accidents, you'll learn your dog's potty signals. Once that starts, pick him up and get him outside or onto paper (or a piddle pad) right away. You also need to understand that he can stop his urine, but once he starts a poop, leave him be. He can't control it and, if you try to move him to a better spot, you'll have a trail to clean up instead of a pile.

There are certain times that all puppies need to go out, so learn these times and avoid accidents.

- Immediately after waking up, in the morning or from a nap
- After any excitement or play
- Within 10-30 minutes of eating
- After a big drink of water
- The absolute last thing before bed at night

Carry the puppy outside to prevent accidents between the crate, or wherever you are, and the doorway. Some pups anticipate a bit too much and they'll go right in front of the door, seconds away from being in the correct spot. So provide 'taxi service' for a little one. Also, unless they're truly desperate (or scared), most puppies won't pee on you. After all, you're Mom and Alpha rolled into one!

Whenever the puppy is inside the home, but cannot be directly supervised, he should be placed in his crate. A good time would be when you're cooking, watching TV, taking a shower or even away from the house for a short period. Take your pup out right before crating him, and again as soon as you let him out of the crate.

Another way to keep your puppy supervised but still be able to do things is to use 'tethering'. Basically you attach him to you via his leash, so he goes where you go. This gives you the freedom to get some housework done. Alternatively, you can tether him to something like a table leg if you're going to be staying in one room of your home, for example, cooking. You need to keep a close eye on him still, and be prepared to drop what you're doing if he shows signs of thinking about going potty. Tethering does, however, give him time outside the crate to stretch, investigate, and learn. It's a great option when you're on the patio or deck, or if you're in the yard. Never let the pup roam unsupervised in the yard, even if it's securely enclosed. They will try to eat anything! I had one little guy who devoured a squished frog, bones and all, before I could stop him, and another who insisted on trying to eat acorns. Needless to say, both experienced severe 'gastric distress.' You also should know that many decorative plants are toxic to dogs.

You definitely want to crate your puppy at bedtime. Sleeping alone is probably a new experience for him, and a slightly scary one. Puppies generally sleep in a pile, the whole litter snuggled close together with their mother. You can ease the transition for your pup by giving him a stuffed toy to curl up with as a fake littermate and, if he's very young, a well-wrapped hot water bottle under the bedding. The ticking of a clock placed nearby can help to mimic the sound of Mom's heartbeat and it reassures many pups. Also, putting a piece of clothing that you've worn into the crate with him can calm his fears since he can cuddle up to your smell. A little consideration for his sudden sense of isolation at night can make it much easier for both of you to get some sleep!

Expect your puppy to have to go potty in the middle of the night for a while, so put his crate in or very near your bedroom if at all possible. He's still a baby after all! It's a good idea if you are proactive about getting him out by setting an alarm clock. Keep whatever shoes, coat, keys, etc., that you'll need when taking him out laid out ready to grab and go for those middle of the night jaunts. Have his leash pre-attached to his collar, so you can just snap the collar on him, or use a slip lead. These trips will only be necessary until he's 5-6 months old. As he gets older, he'll sleep longer, have more control over his bladder, and begin to wake you if he really needs to go. Within a few months, he'll be sleeping through the night without a problem.

The ultimate goal of crate training is to never let your pup go potty in the house. This requires that you (or someone) be there to take him out on time, so you need to fit that into your schedule without fail. If you must be gone more than five hours, use the paper-training method while you are away and set up a managed confinement area with his crate in it.

When done right, there are many advantages to crate training. Crate training can effectively teach a puppy that when the urge to go pee or poop occurs, they are capable of holding it (within their limitations of course). It fits wonderfully with their natural instincts as well. Crate training also strengthens the alpha-pack bond that you are building with your puppy. He is learning that he can rely on you to see to his needs; therefore, he feels he can trust you and have respect for his pack leader. This is the main reason why puppy owners who use crate training have found it to be a quicker way of not only housebreaking their pup, but also teaching other desirable behaviors.

## Litter Pan Training

As mentioned earlier, litter pan training is growing in popularity. Many dogs take to it very well, and it provides an easier cleaner indoor option than just a space on the kitchen floor. For dog owners living in high-rise buildings, people with limited mobility, or dogs who are unsuited for the weather where they live, pan training allows ease and comfort for both owners and dogs. A dog trained to a litter pan will still potty outdoors when going 'walkies,' but he has another option as well. Since little dogs need to go more often than their bigger cousins, it's very helpful for them to have an acceptable indoor area where they can relieve themselves while their owners are away from home. Eight hours for a large dog is like 'holding it' for 24 hours to a little guy! Not a very reasonable expectation.

If a litter pan of some type is your chosen route, make sure you have it ready to go before beginning house-training. Find a convenient spot in your home to place it, and don't move it around except when you need to set up a confinement area. Your puppy needs to learn where to find it! You can relocate it once he's trained.

If your dog is not a toy breed, you'll need to provide a larger pan as he grows. Many people start with a traditional dog litter pan and change to a round one, since dogs like to circle before pooping. For a larger dog, this could even be something like a 'kiddie pool', perhaps moved into the garage or basement after he's trained.

Make sure that your dog can easily enter the pan without climbing or jumping. It needs to be simple for him to get in and out! You may need to cut the entryway down a bit lower so that he can step in. Some people like the pellets that are sold as litter, and there are several different types, and others just use a piddle pad in the pan. If your pup doesn't seem to like it, or tries to eat it, change to a different type of absorbing medium. [Cat litter doesn't work very well for most dogs because it really gets stuck in their feet.] The fake grass models have a tray underneath which collects the urine, but many folks like to line that with wee wee pads for quicker, easier cleaning.

Be aware, if you're not already, that although young male pups squat, as he matures he'll lift his leg to urinate. By that time you need to make provisions so that he doesn't pee over the top of the pan or onto the wall. You can purchase posts or little plastic fire hydrants, scented with attractant, to give him something to aim at, or use a pan with higher sides. If you have multiple dogs, you may need multiple pans. They sometimes don't want to share and won't use a pan that's already been soiled.

To train your pup to a litter pan, follow the same procedures as crate training. You just take the pup to the litter pan instead of taking him outside to the yard. If you need to be away for a while, set up a confinement area with the litter pan inside, just as you would do with paper training. Be sure to cover the rest of the floor with paper (in case of accidents) until your pooch is reliable with the pan!

Just as with newspaper, pads, and even the yard, the litter pan should be kept as clean as possible. Clean up messes as soon as possible, and change the litter following the instructions that come with it. Empty the pan for a thorough cleansing with disinfectant cleaner at least once a week, and hose off the plastic turf as well.

## Crazy Training Plan

If you would like to streamline the housebreaking process, and you can completely free yourself from any other responsibilities, work or family, for a couple of days, then this 'extreme' method might be just the thing for you. It's very effective and creates a strong bond, but it does take its toll on you.

The 'crazy' way to house-train your pup, within his physical bladder limits of course, is to be completely proactive. The pup never goes on the floor, not once. How do you achieve this miracle, you ask? With self-sacrifice and a total focus on the task, allowing no distractions. It's just you, puppy, and housebreaking.

This will work with a litter pan or a pad as well as going outdoors. It's actually a simple procedure, a sort of 'extreme crate training,' but you have to 'suck it up' and follow through—that's the craziness. It's 24/7 on your part until you reach his physical limits. After that, you never ask him to exceed those limits.

Still with me? Then here's how it goes. You bring puppy home and let him potty before you bring him inside. Ten minutes later, you take him out again (or take him to the pan or pad). Praise a successful trip! If he doesn't go, give him another ten minutes and then out again. After each successful potty break, you add five minutes to the time between trips, so you'd wait 15 minutes and then go out again. After each unsuccessful trip, repeat the same interval.

You need to continue this all day and all night, following and adjusting the schedule. Wake up (use an alarm), wake him up (really), and go out. (I slept on the sofa by the door to facilitate the process, while puppy slept tethered on the floor next to me.) Work some playtime in between some of the trips, and don't forget to wedge in some food for both you and the pup. Watch some TV together. But keep track of the time! You'll become a little zombie-like, but that's OK. Think of it as a short-term extreme sporting event. Stay focused on your mission!

A three-month-old pup will settle into a 3-4 hour maximum interval between trips. Once you know what that limit is for your pup, you can make arrangements to let him relieve himself within that interval. You can also crate him and crawl into bed until your next puppy potty break (set the alarm!).

Although you'll need about a day to fully recover, depending on what time of day you brought him home and started the process, you'll also have a very accurate idea of his bathroom habits and needs. You will have learned his potty rituals—does he sniff or circle, or both? (This can help you prevent future 'accidents' if he needs to go earlier than usual for some reason.) You've earned his trust, and he can count on you to meet, even anticipate, his needs. He's never eliminated anywhere except where you, his pack leader, have approved, so he won't be inclined to start. Even young as he is, he'll come to you for a potty break. And, in spite of the sleep disruption, it is time spent working together that can give you a very strong bond with your dog. Packs work cooperatively for the good of all, and that's what you two have just done together!

The follow-up is simply assuring that you never expect him, or force him, to exceed his capabilities. You get him to his designated area within his time limit, period. If you can't be there to do it, then you find someone who can help you out. This means at night, too! Set the alarm, take him for his potty break, praise, and go back to bed. Once he's 6 months old or so and has full control of himself, he'll be extremely reliable (and sleeping through the night).

# Chapter 5    Training Words And Body Language

• Sharp and short word: When picking a word to use, one of the first things you'll want to consider is that the word you're using is both a short word as well as a sharp word. The reason your word choice should be short and sharp is that you want your puppy to be able to easily distinguish that word from the rest of the words you say on a consistent basis in order for them to turn on their listening ears when you say it. Since our words are generally a stream with a flow, having a word that you say much more sharply will get their attention a lot easier. Having a word that is short will also make it easier to say in the moment, as opposed to messing up that word and therefore confusing your puppy.

• Easy to say at the right time: The next qualification you'll want to consider when choosing a command word is whether or not that word will be easy to say in the moment that your dog is performing a negative behavior. It can be fun to choose a word that is silly or different to use as a command and can be hard to use in the moment. For example, if you teach your puppy something like the word "desist" when you want them to stop, it may be hard to recall quickly in the moment the command needs to be applied. For this reason, it is much easier to choose a simpler word for the command. When choosing a word, think of the first thing that would come to your mind when going to use that command. That way, you will not need to put too much thought into the command you use when it needs to be quickly applied.

• Use words that aren't often used: Another thing you should consider when choosing a word to use for each command is making sure that it isn't a word that you'll use in day to day life too often especially in front of your dog. The reason for this is that hearing a word too often when not being used as a prompt for them will cause that word to weaken and it may start to become meaningless to your puppy when they hear it used. For example, if you're a person that says "okay" often to your family members or while talking on the phone, you'll want to avoid using it as a command to tell your dog that they may stop what they're doing. Since this is a word you use often, you may either be accidentally prompting your dog to end a command when you don't yet want them to and can even cause them to not pay attention or notice when you do say that word to them. For that reason, you should choose a word for each command that won't be overused in your diction.

• Finding balance: Reading through the last two suggestions for finding a word to prompt your puppy for a command, you may find yourself confused. If you shouldn't use a word that isn't commonly used and you shouldn't use a word that you do use often, what words are the right ones to use? The answer to that question is to do your best to find some balance and find a word that falls somewhere in the middle of those descriptions. This perfect word will be something that comes naturally to you when the command needs to be used but not so naturally that it's an everyday part of the way you speak. This may require some trial and error in order to perfect but with some trial and planning you should be able to find the proper words to use for each command. The only exception is if you're very serious and adamant about training your puppy and don't want to risk confusing them at all, in which case you may choose to use words in a different language that they will not otherwise hear. This, though, will require much more effort and attention in order to properly follow through on.

Applying Verbal Commands

Now that you've decided on the words that you will use for each different command, you will need to learn how to properly apply each command while teaching your dog how to perform the action that you're requesting of them. You'll always want to do the standard of saying your command word followed by a marker and often a treat immediately after they perform that action. However, here are some of the best ways in order to train your dog to respond to specific verbal cues.

• Sitting with verbal cues: The first step to teaching your puppy to sit with verbal cues is to put the treat that you're using near their nose so they can smell and acknowledge the treat. You'll then want to lift the treat up towards the top of your puppy's head while saying the command 'sit' or whichever word you've chosen for this command. Generally, your dog's head will follow this treat and they will lower their rear end to the ground. Once your puppy's bum touches the ground, you'll want to give them a treat as well as utilize your verbal marker. If your puppy backs up instead, you may try this again with a wall behind your puppy. If, however, your puppy stands up, you may want to lower the treat as you are likely holding it up too high.

• Laying down with verbal cues: When teaching your puppy how to lay down, you'll want to move the treat close to your puppy's face, then continue to move that treat straight down towards the floor. After doing this, you'll want to slowly move this treat towards the floor while using the verbal cue you've chosen to have your pup lay down. Your puppy will ideally follow this treat down, which you will then reward with praise and a treat. Since this command is essentially a two-part movement, it may take a few tries in order to get your puppy to do it accurately.

• Standing with verbal cues: In order to teach your puppy how to stand using verbal cues, you'll need to first get your puppy into a sitting position. Once your pup is in a sitting position, you'll want to put the treat in front of their nose and slowly move that treat towards your body while giving your chosen command for them to stand. For a visual, this movement should look similar to how it would look to open up a dresser drawer. Your puppy should then follow this treat by standing up, which you will then reward with your positive marker as well as a treat.

• Sitting from down position with verbal cues: Lastly, we'll go over how to get your puppy from a laying down position into a sitting position. When your puppy is laying down, you'll want to put the treat in front of their nose and slowly raise that treat up over their head while giving your command for sit. Your puppy will likely follow this treat into a sitting position, which you will then reward with your verbal marker as well as a treat.

Teaching your dog to obey commands isn't just done to impress other people, although it is definitely a plus. No, basic commands like Sit, Stay, and Come are actually crucial because they can help save your dog's life. For example, your dog is on the other side of the road and wants to run to your side – commanding him to sit and stay would ensure that he doesn't run recklessly. So how do you teach all these? Here's how:

## Sit

Sit is the easiest command you can teach your dog because it's a perfectly natural position for them. At some point, your dog will sit down and all you have to do is foster the association between the position and the command. There are two ways of doing this:

- First, you can wait for the dog to sit naturally and then say "Sit!". Repeat the words once or twice, making sure he stays in that particular position. Wait a beat and then provide the treat. Do this every time you catch the dog moving from the standing to sitting position.

- Assist the dog into the sitting position by putting pressure on his rump and pushing it downwards so that he is forced to sit down. Utter the command again, wait for a few seconds and then give the treat.

Make sure that the dog stays sitting when he gets the treat. If he chooses to stand up while reaching for the food, take it away and push him back to the sitting position, doing so gently but insistently.

If you have a clicker, this would also be an excellent way to let your dog know that he is doing the right thing. Every time he moves from stand to sit, click the clicker. This tells him that *this* is the action you're rewarding him for. Do this for all other training sessions when you're introducing something new.

Stay

Stay is a command best taught when your dog already knows about Sit. To do this, coax your dog into the Sit position and give the "Stay" command. Take one step backward, clicking the clicker as you go to tell the dog that you want him to remain in the sitting position. Take at least 3 steps backwards, clicking the clicker each time. If the pup stays in place, you can now praise him and offer a treat. Note that it's usually best for you to go to the dog instead of him going to you during the Stay lesson. This way, you'll find it easier to teach the Come command.

Note that most dogs will start to walk forward when you walk backwards. When they do this, order them into the sitting position again and start from the top, making sure the "Stay" command is said clearly and in a powerful manner. You can try just taking one step back and adding to the distance as the pup learns the command.

Come

When you've taught Stay, Come is the next command the dog should learn. Obviously, dogs naturally go to their master but when out in public, it's crucial that the dog goes directly to you after being given the command. To do this, give the "Stay" command and slowly walk farther and farther from your dog. Instead of going back to him for the treat however, you stay put, utter the "Come" command and let him walk up to you. Click the clicker as he walks forward so he knows that this is exactly what you want.

Walking on a Leash

Leash walking is so much more than taking your dog out for a stroll in public. From the way a dog and master handle the leash, you can tell exactly how the relationship between them goes. During leash walking, the dog must not pull forward but walk sedately beside or behind their owner.

For beginners, the leash must be kept short – just enough distance between your hand and the dog's collar with possibly a few inches of leeway. This gives you excellent control, letting the dog know exactly where you want to go while preventing him from wandering around.

Whenever the pooch starts to pull on the leash, stop walking entirely. When he calms down, you can start walking again – letting the dog know that YOU are in charge and that when you stop, so must he. Do this repeatedly and make sure to always move forward, confident in your stride so that the dog can absorb that confidence.

You won't perfect leash walking immediately, but you'll find that by sticking to this technique, the dog catches on and becomes more willing. Your aim is for the pooch to walk continuously, head forward, and tail in its natural relaxed position.

# Chapter 6       Basic Training - Common Commands

This chapter is where we get to some of the fun stuff about training! We are going to look at some of the steps that you can take in order to teach your puppy some basic commands. There are a lot of different commands that you are able to teach your puppy, but we are going to focus on some of the basic ones that will make your life with your puppy a little bit easier. Some of the basic commands that we need to take a look at include:

## Sit

Teaching your puppy how to sit can be a stepping stone to making sure that the puppy is a well-trained dog. When the puppy can sit on command, it helps them to learn some self-control. This method of teaching your puppy to sit is going to teach them how to sit down physically, but can be a good way for the puppy to learn how to calm down mentally and engage their focus on you. Before you try moving on to any other trick or command, make sure that your puppy has mastered sitting. Some steps that you can use to help with the teaching of the sit command includes:

1. Have the puppy face you. Tell the puppy to "sit" while you hold out a treat in the hand position of your choice.
2. After saying sit once, you are not going to repeat the word again.
3. Put the treat to the nose of your puppy.
4. Move the hand so that it goes slowly forward, from the direction you are in, towards the dog as if you are going to move the treat over the head of the puppy.  The reason that we do this is that it is an automatic way to get the puppy to lower their butt as they try to get to the treat.
5. Once the puppy has their butt on the floor, you can reward them using the treat and the clicker word.
6. During this process, it is important for you to go at the pace of your puppy, and you need to keep the treat on their nose. Also, never force the puppy to sit down by pushing their butt onto the floor. This isn't going to teach the puppy anything since you are forcing it, and it

can cause some harm to the hips of the puppy if you are too forceful.

7. In the next fifteen to twenty minutes, repeat this exercise as many times as the puppy will do it to help reinforce the command.

As you go through this process, do not start to feel discouraged if the puppy is not sitting down the first time you do it. Some puppies don't realize what is going on and that they need to lower their butt to get the treat. But patience and persistence is the best way for you to get them to start listening to you. If the puppy starts to give up on the treat and doesn't seem like they are focused any longer, saying their name or using a kissy noise can be a good way to get their attention back on you.

## Lay Down

After you and your puppy have worked on the sit command for a bit, and the puppy has got this part mastered, it is time to move on to a second command of lay down. You must make sure that the puppy knows how to sit before you start working with the lay down command because if you start teaching them too many commands at once, then you are just going to add in some confusion to the mix.

When the puppy is ready to learn how to lay down, get them to sit in front of you. Next, hold the treat in one hand, and then using the other hand, signal the puppy to lay down by using a hand gesture that had your pointer finger pointing down to the ground in front of the puppy's face. Some of the other steps that you need to use to work on the laying down command include:

1. Put the treat that you are using up to the nose of the puppy and then start to slowly lure the puppy down. You can do this by moving the hand down to the floor, somewhere between their paws. Go at the pace for your dog.

2. Once your hand with the treat hits the floor, slowly move it towards you and away from him along the floor. This motion should be enough to get the dog to lower themselves into a laying position.

3. Once you are able to get the puppy to lay down all of the way, make sure to say the clicker word and give them a treat.

4. Repeat this exercise as many times as you can in the next 15 minutes to help the puppy get the idea down.

Keep in mind with this one that the laying down command is going to force your puppy to focus a bit longer before they are able to get the treat that they want. There are going to be times when the puppy wants to give up before you are able to finish with the final position. Don't get frustrated with this; just keep trying, and your puppy will start to catch on to what you want them to do.

## Stay

Teaching your puppy how to stay where you want, even when they want to run off and do something else, is a great training tool that you should work on once the puppy learns how to sit and lay down. It is also a command that can take some time to learn, so bring on the patience. Think of how much self-control you have to teach to a small puppy, and how long they need to maintain their attention span in order to actually stay put when you want them to.

There are different methods that you can use for this one, but sometimes it is easiest to get the puppy to stay when you have them in the lay down position. This means that they are going to be less likely to want to move when they can lay all the way down rather than sitting, but you definitely can teach this command in either position.

The hand position that we need to work with for the stay command is to put your hand up, palm facing the puppy, and fingers together. Think of the hand position that you would use when trying to stop someone from coming towards you. Once you have the hand position and have used the command "stay" to the puppy, the other steps to this process that you need to follow includes:

1. With your hand out, take a step back using both feet.
2. After the two steps back, return back to the position you were at to start.
3. If your puppy was good and stayed seated that entire time, reward them with a treat and with the clicker word.
    1. Keep in mind that this is a puppy, and they probably will not want to stay still. If your puppy does get up before you can return to them, tell them "uh-uh" and get them to go back into the seated position.
    2. For the first few sessions, this may be as far as you are able to get. And that is just fine.

The puppy naturally wants to follow you. Just work with them until you can get them to stay seated the whole time.

4. Once the puppy stays seated, try taking two steps back and then returning before the reward and the clicker word.

5. Keep increasing the distance that you decide to walk away from the pup, seeing how long you can go away before they start getting up again. Do this until the puppy starts to understand the command that you are giving them.

6. Repeat this exercise many times until the puppy learns how to stay put.

## Wait

After you are done teaching your puppy how to stay, it is time to teach them how to wait. This is a very useful command that you can work with, but often it is underused. It can be applied to teaching your puppy to wait for their food, wait to get their leash off, wait to get out of the crate, and more. It is a great way to teach your puppy a bit of self-control and patience, which is something that all dog owners need at some point or another.

Teaching self-control to the puppy is going to be the key to having a dog that is well trained and can do a great job with all the areas of obedience. Definitely take some time to teach your puppy how to listen to this command. When you are ready to start with, it put the puppy in the position that you would like them to wait in. You may find that sitting or lying down is going to work for this. The best hand signals to use here is to have your pointer finger going up. The steps that you can use to make this happen includes:

1. Tell your puppy to wait and then use the wait hand signal.
2. While the puppy is in the seated position, preferably in the crate where feedings are supposed to happen. Slowly lower the food bowl down to where they can eat.
3. If the puppy sees the bowl of food and starts to jump up or get at the food in other ways, you raise the bowl back up while saying "uh-uh."
4. Get the puppy back into the seated position and then start again. If the puppy is younger or has a lot of energy, you may have to repeat these steps a few times in order to get them to listen to you.

1. Do not set the bowl of food all the way down until the puppy has actually patiently waited for you to lower it without them getting away from the seated position. Be aware that this can take a bit of time.

5. After you have been able to set the food bowl down, see if you are able to get the puppy to wait for another second, and then say, "OK."

    1. If you see that the puppy starts to go for the food before you say the word "OK," you can tell them "uh-uh" and pick up the bowl before trying again.

    2. "OK" is going to be the release word for your puppy, and it will tell them that it is now fine to stop waiting, and they can eat the food that is in front of them.

    3. As you go through this process, you will want to lengthen the amount of time that the puppy is going to wait between setting the bowl down and saying OK. This takes a bit longer but will get the puppy used to waiting until you give the orders to do something.

## Come

The next command that we are going to look at is the one to come. When you do this one, you are going to teach your puppy how to come when you call them. This is also one that a lot of pet owners are going to forget to teach, and it can lead to some issues with the puppy not listening to you. This is a foundational command that you should work with your puppy on for years to come. You may use it to keep the puppy near you, when there is danger, and more.

Be prepared for this one to take a bit longer than some of the other ones. The puppy has to let you move away from them and then has to move to meet you. There are a number of steps that this will entail working with, but this is a great one to focus your attention on and make sure that you can get them to really listen to you. When you are ready to teach your puppy this command, you can follow these steps:

1. When you are working with this command, make sure that you start out in an enclosed area. This makes it easier in case your puppy decides not to listen because they are limited in the space they have to run away.

2. Take your puppy off the leash and allow them to have some time to just explore and roam around.

3. When you are ready, say the name of the puppy and then use the command "Come" in a positive voice, while also holding on to a treat.

   1. Keep in mind that you want to associate this command with positivity.

   2. Your goal is to get the dog to come every time that you call them. For this to happen, the puppy needs to be conditioned to think that something positive is going to happen when they come to you.

4. If your puppy doesn't end up coming over to you right away, that is fine. You can make some kissy noises or do another thing that will get their attention to make sure that they see the treat that you are offering. Be patient here and work on redirecting the attention of the puppy until he comes to you.

5. When the puppy does come to you, make sure that you reward them with the treat, as well as the clicker word. Do this even if it took a long time for the puppy to make their way over to

you. They did listen, even if it took longer than you wanted.

6.     Repeat this exercise many times until the puppy starts to come right over to you.

**Leave It**

The next command that we need to take a look at is "leave it." This can be a beneficial command to train your puppy, considering that they often like to be adventurous and get into everything. When you decide to use this command when the puppy is heading towards something that you don't want them to be in, you are going to see some great results. As the puppy wants to explore and see things, there are many times when this kind of command is going to be a good one to use.

Now, there are going to be a few methods that you are able to use when it comes to the command of "leave it." The first method is going to follow the steps below to make things happen.

1. Any time that the puppy starts to go for or is already into something that you want them to leave alone, firmly tell the puppy "leave it."

2. Remember to only tell them the command once. You can use their name or another sound to get their attention.

3. If you find that the puppy is not responding to this, put a treat or some other toy on their nose and lure them over to listening to you.

4. Once the puppy does decide to leave the object, tell them "Yes" and use the clicker word of your choice. A reward is a good way to reinforce this idea, as well.

5. Remember that your reward for this one needs to be really motivating. You are trying to get the puppy to leave something alone that they are interested in. If the reward is not good, then they are more likely to ignore you and go after the other thing.

The above method is going to work well for most puppies, and it is definitely one you can work with. But another option that you may want to try working with as well depending on your puppy and whether or not they respond to the first method is the second method we will tell you about below:

1. Have the puppy start this training session by lying down.

2. Put down a treat on the ground, covering it by your hand if necessary.
3. Tell your pup to "leave it."
4. Once the puppy looks at you rather than the treat, tell them "Yes" and reward them with the treat from the other hand.
5. Remember, you need to practice this one a bit. It is going to help the dog realize that if they leave the first thing, they are going to get something better, which makes them respond better to you.

**Touch**

Touch can be a great command to work with, and it is almost like a trick that you are able to do with your puppy. Touch is going to be a great way to teach your puppy to target something and then touch it with their nose. It is a good way to get the brain of your puppy to move and even to keep their focus when it is needed. Some of the steps that you are going to be able to use in order to teach your puppy how to respond to the touch command will include:

1. Make sure that you sit down with the puppy facing you.

2. Hold a treat or some other reward in your one hand.

3. Command your dog to "Touch" and then hold out the hand that doesn't have the treat, so it is flat in front of the nose of your dog while holding onto the treat in the other hand.

    1. Once the puppy starts to get the hang of this kind of command, it will no longer be necessary to have the treat in your hand, and you can just put the hand where you would like.

4. In the beginning, you want to put the touching hand six inches or so away from the nose of your dog.

5. As soon as you are able to get the nose of your dog to touch your hand, you can reward him with the treat you have and the clicker word you choose to use.

6. You should never give your dog the treat in the hand that you want them to touch.

7. If you find that the dog is getting the hang of this trick pretty quickly, you can remove the treat and no longer use it at all.

8. As you progress with your puppy, keep moving your touching hand higher above the nose of your dog, adding in a bit of difficulty with it.

## Shake

Now we are going to move a bit more into some of the different tricks that you are able to do when you work with your puppy. But the way that you do this is going to be pretty similar to the commands that we were doing before. Think of how much fun it is going to be when you want to get your puppy to shake your hand.

You will find that most puppies are going to take some time to learn how to do this trick. But if you have already spent some time teaching them some of the other commands, it may be a bit easier. As always, your job is to be patient and persistent with this and work on it each day until your puppy is ready to go with it. Some of the steps that you are able to use in order to teach your puppy how to shake with you include:

1. Make sure that you begin this with the puppy facing you.
2. Use the command "shake" and make the shake hand gesture with your hand out, palm out, and waiting.

3. Place the treat right up to one side of your pup's chest.

    1. This one is going to take a bit of patience and can be harder for the puppy to figure out what exactly you want them to do.

    2. Most pups are going to try to bite at the treat and will take some extra pains in order to get to the treat.

4. As soon as the puppy starts to paw at the treat, or even if they just start to lift the paw, immediately reward them with the treat and the clicker word.

For this kind of exercise, if you find that your pup is standing up and getting out of the seated position that you put them in, this is fine. Once they figure out that they are able to get the reward when they lift up their paw, they will figure out that it is easier for them to lift up the paw while they are seated. However, when you first start with this exercise, begin it with the puppy in the seated position before you begin.

**Heel**

The next command that is on our list is going to be heel. Teaching your puppy how to heel can be one of the most beneficial skills that you can teach them. If you are able to focus on this command with them when they are young, they will know how to behave when you get them older. One big behavioral problem that can happen with a puppy or dog when they get older is that they will pull on the leash while walking. Teaching your puppy how to heel is going to avoid this issue and can make walking a bit easier.

Before we get into some of the steps that we need to take in order to teach your puppy how to heel, we need to look at some tips for loose leash walking. First, remember to work with positive reinforcement. You also want to walk with a leash that is loose and never tighten it because this puts some strain on either end of the leash. You also should consider being as consistent as possible with what side your puppy needs to walk on. Pick a side and keep them there.

With these two things in mind, it is time to see how you can teach your puppy when and how to heel at the right time. The steps to making this happen will include:

1. Position the leash, so it is on your arm or wrist, but make sure that it is still a bit loose.
2. If you have the puppy on the right side, make sure to hold onto the end of the leash with

your left hand, and grab it with the right hand down by your side. If you are holding onto the puppy on the left side, then you can flip these instructions around.

3. If you find that the puppy will stay near your side the whole time, then the second hand on the leash won't be necessary.

4. Get into a position where your puppy is on the side that you choose, and then get their attention.

5. Your goal with this one, if you can, is to get the puppy to be as calm and focused as possible so that they can pay attention to the command that you use. Have the puppy sit by you and then reward with the treat and the clicker word.

6. Say the name of your puppy and then ask them to "heel." Keep looking at the puppy as you continue to walk.

7. Any time that the puppy looks up at you, you should say the clicker word. Depending on how often the puppy looks at you, you can provide them with a treat with the clicker word or just on occasion.

1. The more that you see the puppy look up at you, the less you should reward with a treat so that you can slowly wean off this.

8. When it is time, take one step forward and see if you can get the attention of your puppy. Ideally, they are going to stay next to you and will heel rather than trying to pull forward.

   1. If you find that the puppy is losing their focus on you at any time, say their name or use the kissy noise, but never repeat the command more than once.

   2. If the puppy keeps the focus on you and the leash is loose, keep on walking. If the puppy tightens the leash and pulls forward, then stop with the walking.

9. Your goal here is to get the puppy to walk back over to you and get the leash loose. If the puppy doesn't do this, say their name and get their attention. If they still don't come back to you, take a step back, and see if the puppy will follow you. Last case scenario that they aren't listening to you, then lure them back with a treat.

10. Once the puppy is back to you again, use the clicker word and offer a treat. Repeat this exercise a bunch of times until the puppy is able to learn how to listen to you and do what you are asking with the heeling.

You want to make sure that with this one that you are picking out a treat that your puppy really likes. Your goal with heel is to teach the puppy how to listen to you and stop moving or pulling on the leash. This means that the reward needs to be greater than whatever else may be catching their attention at the time. Go all out with this one and pick out some of the best treats to get the puppy to listen to you.

There are some puppies who struggle with heel because they are resistant to working with the leash. If this is your puppy, then you should consider working with a harness when teaching the puppy how to heel, and even when you want to introduce them to leash walking in general. Most puppies and older dogs are going to respond to the harness so much better than using the leash for heeling, and for working with the leash for walking in any form.

There are a lot of different commands that you are able to work with when it is time to teach your puppy how to listen to you. Most of these are critical commands that can get the puppy to listen to what you want them to do and to keep them out of harm, though a few of them can be almost like fun tricks that you can do together. Make sure that you take your time and go at the speed that works the best for your puppy. They will learn if you are consistent with the treats and continue doing the rewards and the clicker word each time that they succeed in doing what you would like.

# Chapter 7     Top Techniques To Train

Now that you have learned all the fundamental knowledge when it comes to puppy care, behavior and different types of training, it's time to learn the actual techniques in training. In this chapter, we will be going through the three puppy training techniques, the most notably effective and common ones in the industry. By now, you should have a good understanding of dog and puppy behaviors and be able to choose the best training technique for your specific dog. The techniques we will be discussing are; Positive Reinforcement Technique, Clicker Training, and the Alpha Dog technique. These techniques are well suited to help puppies learn quickly and efficiently. In our next book, we will be focusing on other less popular techniques that are aimed to help adult dogs rather than puppies. Let's get started with learning what these techniques are, how they work, and the benefits they bring.

Positive Reinforcement

The positive reinforcement technique is proven to be the most effective and most commonly used puppy training technique presently. The theory behind this technique is extremely simple; dogs will repeat good behavior when it is rewarded for it. If they showcase bad behavior, there will be no reward or any acknowledgment at all. The 'punishment' in this technique will be in the form of no reward or rewards taken away. There is no need for any harsh or physical punishment whatsoever.

The way positive reinforcement works is by rewarding your dog with a treat every single time they do the desired command or behavior that you are asking for. The trick here is that you need to present the reward within seconds of your dog's completed action so your dog is able to associate that action with a reward. More skilled trainers will actually pair the positive reinforcement technique with clicker training. The clicker helps show the dog the exact moment of when their action or behavior has been completed. During positive reinforcement training, the commands that you are using to direct your dog must be short and concise. For example, 'sit', 'down', 'drop it', as opposed to 'sit down!' or 'Hey! Drop it!'. When you are training a young puppy it is important to keep an eye out on all of their behavior and begin rewarding the ones that you deem as good. I suggest investing in a portable treat bag that you can carry around with you at all times. This way, once you see your puppy performing a good behavior like lying down calmly next to your feet, you can reward him/her with a treat right away. If you are waiting too long to provide a reward to your puppy, it will become ineffective as your puppy may associate the reward with a different action. A good rule to follow here is to give your puppy a reward as soon as they finish the command. Some professionals even advise giving the reward right before they finish the command. See what works best with your pup and stick to it!

The most important element in the positive reinforcement technique is consistency. If you and your pup live in a home with other people, everyone needs to participate in using the same commands and the same reward system. At the beginning of your puppy's training, present him/her with a reward every time the desired action is completed. When your puppy has fully learned the action and aces it every time, you may begin to reward that specific action intermittently. Be careful of accidentally rewarding your dog during bad behavior. For example, some people will try to get their dog to stop barking by luring their attention away by offering a treat. It is effective in ceasing the barking since your dog is distracted by the reward but this will actually teach your dog that barking will generate a treat/reward. Instead of using a treat to get your dog's attention, give him a command instead that will help calm him/her down. For example, if your dog is barking relentlessly give him/her a command such as 'down'. It is a lot more difficult for your dog to bark when they are lying down. Once he/she completes this command, you can then reward him/her. Remember to never offer rewards while your dog is performing bad behavior!

We used to give treats as the main reward when it comes to positive reinforcement training but you can actually use treats, toys, pets, and praise as a substitute. In the early stages of dog training, it can be really easy to overfeed your puppy if you are using treats as a reward. Make sure to use small treats if you are rewarding with food to minimize the calories given to your dog. You can break down larger treats into smaller pieces yourself if you aren't able to find a smaller size. Once your dog has learned a certain behavior or specific command completely, start to change your reward system for that specific action to an intermittent reward. From there you can change the reward system entirely for that specific action to praise instead, and only give treats as a reward if they are learning a new action/behavior. Consistency is the key to success when it comes to this technique. Be very disciplined with your puppy and make sure you are ready to reward your pup when they perform good behavior. Just like most things in life, only completing something once won't make you an expert.

Clicker Training

We mentioned clicker training briefly during the subchapter of positive reinforcement. This is actually because clicker training relies on the exact same fundamentals as positive reinforcement. Some people may even tell you that clicker training and positive reinforcement are the same technique. The premise of clicker training is that it uses a clicker device to make a loud and brief noise. This noise will be an indication to the dog that they have accomplished the desired action/behavior.

The differentiating factor and also clicker training's biggest benefit is the fact that it is able to notify your puppy the exact moment of which he/she has completed the desired action or behavior. After that, you follow with a reward. This is extremely important as your dog will be conditioned through this type of training that a click means a reward.

Clicker training is most effective when you are trying to teach your dog new actions or behaviors. It can also help change the basic actions or behaviors that your dog already knows into more difficult ones. Clicker training is actually the most popular method that professional dog trainers use. Although this method is incredibly effective in teaching your dog wanted behaviors and actions, it does not do much for curbing undesired behaviors.

Below I will provide you with 15 tips on clicker training. If you are a new dog owner, you should be able to learn this technique fairly quickly as it is not extremely difficult. The most difficult part of it is the time and discipline it requires. You can easily purchase a clicker at your local pet store.

1. The first tip is to test out how your clicker works. In most clickers, there should be a very obvious button for you to press. Press the button and if you hear a click that is two-toned, then you have succeeded. This will be the click that you use as an indication that your dog has completed the action you requested.
2. Press the button on the clicker right after your puppy has completed the desired behavior. Timing is crucial because if you don't use the clicker right after the action, your puppy may have difficulty associating the clicker with the action. Once you have used the clicker, you may present your puppy with a reward. The timing of the reward is not as important here.

3. You can use clicker any time that your dog does behavior that is good. You don't necessarily need to give a command before using the clicker. If your dog sits down on its own, use the clicker right away and present him/her with a reward.

4. If you are trying to showcase positive enthusiasm, do not increase the number of clicks but increase the number of treats.

5. Try to keep your practice sessions short and sweet. Puppies tend to learn more in a 5-minute window compared to a one hour window. If you do a few 5-minute sessions each day, you will generate significant results.

6. You can fix bad behavior by clicking at good behavior. Instead of punishing your puppy if you catch him/her peeing inside, click and provide extra rewards when your puppy is peeing outside.

7. Use the clicker for movements that are voluntary or accidental but is still towards the requested goal. Try to encourage your dog into the movement that you are asking but don't physically help them do it. Let your pup discover the behavior by themselves and then click and reward if they completed it successfully.

8. You don't always have to click when your pup has completed a behavior perfectly. You can also click and reward for the small movements towards the desired behavior. For instance, if you are teaching your dog to sit, you may use the clicker when your dog begins to crouch.

9. You may begin raising your goal once your dog is more skilled at the basic behaviors. For instance, if your dog has mastered 'down' and is lying down, you can ask him to lie down longer. Wait a few seconds longer than you would normally click. This is called 'shaping' technique.

10. Your pup will soon learn that a click means a reward and he/she may begin to show you desired behaviors spontaneously. Your dog will try to get you to use the clicker to achieve a reward. If this is the case, you may not introduce a 'cue'. The cue can be a hand signal or a word. You can use the clicker when your dog completes the desired behavior after the cue. If your dog is successful at it, then you can provide the reward. Start to ignore your dog's spontaneous behavior if he/she has not been given a cue.

11.        Clicker training is not a type of training that is based on commands. It is ineffective to order your pup around. If you notice that your dog isn't responding to your cues properly don't treat it as disobeying but instead, it is likely that your dog hasn't learned what the cue is yet. If you have other animals in the house, try to do training sessions separately to avoid confusion.

12.        If you have selected clicker training to be your technique of choice, always carry your clicker around. This way, you'd be able to catch good behaviors like sitting down quietly or peeing outside to help them learn that those behaviors are good. Then, you can associate a cue with it.

13.        Avoid being angry or negative when using clicker training. If you are upset at your pet, avoid using the clicker. Make sure you are not mixing up your clicker with scoldings otherwise your pet may lose confidence in the entire system.

14.        If there is a behavior that you think you are not making progress with, it could be that you are clicking too late. Try to use the clicker right before your dog completes the desired behavior. If you are

still struggling with the timing, try asking someone else to watch you and to help you click.

15.          Make sure you are having fun throughout this training! This is a great way to bond with your puppy and you will be surprised at how fast they can learn.

Alpha Dog

The Alpha Dog technique relies on using the instinctual pack mentality within wild dogs. This technique is also known as dominance training. The basis of this relies completely on the natural relationship of dominance and submission with canines. The theory is that dogs will naturally follow their social hierarchy without question. It is very common that our domestic puppy may see themselves as alpha and will need to learn that the alpha is actually their human and not them. To be able to use this method, you will need to have a good understanding of your puppy's body language, communication, and the ability to respond properly by utilizing your authority and confidence.

If this is going to be your technique of choice, you need to lay a few ground rules for you and your pup. Firstly, your dog will be forbidden to sit or sleep on any furniture with you. You should not kneel down to your dog's eye level. Those are all signs to your dog that you guys are equals in the relationship. You must showcase dominant body language to your dog. Some people may think that this is too harsh but keep in mind that all your dog sees is the natural hierarchy system. Your dog won't see this as 'mean' but will actually give you the respect of an alpha.

Let's dig a little bit deeper into this technique. Since you are the alpha and the leader of the pack, you always go first. If you live with other people in your home, they are also the alphas. The people all get to eat first, go out first, and sit down first. If your dog is trying to sit before you, you can command them to 'sit' or 'down'. If your dog is asking you for something, you have to make him/her work for it. For instance, if your dog is wanting to go outside, give him/her a command and have them complete it before you let them out. Secondly, you need to show your dog that you are always in charge as the alpha. If you are having a meal, command your dog to go to their designated spot such as their doggy bed. In a wild dog pack, the alpha is never disturbed by other members when they are eating. You will need to teach your dog to not watch you as you or other people are eating.

Alpha training is useful if your dog is under the mindset that they are the alpha of the home. Bear in mind that not only male dogs can take on the role of alpha, but females can also do that as well. When we allow our dogs to sleep and sit with us on furniture, they will consider themselves as equal and cause them to believe that they are the alpha. There is a possibility that this may manifest and lead to aggressive or dominant behaviors.

# Chapter 8    Physical    And    Mental Exercises

Once your puppy is leash trained, walking him is an enjoyable way for the two of you to bond and provides you with time to clear your mind and get some exercise, too.

**The Normal Puppy**

An untrained puppy isn't aware of the dangers around him. He will strain against his leash, and he'll hate that he can't get free. He'll buck, jump, and do anything he can to get out of his harness or collar. He'll also want to stop and smell everything he can. A puppy gets a lot of information from his sense of smell, and he can tell if something is good or bad, if another animal has been around, or even if it's just interesting to him.

**Introduce the Collar**

There are dozens of different collar and leash styles to choose from, and the best one for you will depend on your dog. Small dogs do well in a harness so they can't slip out of their collars. That works well for puppies of all breeds.

When you first introduce the collar to your pup, be sure it fits properly. There should be enough room for you to fit two fingers between the collar and your pup's neck. Make putting the collar on fun by using an upbeat, but calm voice and reward your pup with a treat once the collar is fastened. Some puppies will try to push the collar off or scratch at it; after all, it is a new sensation.

## Introduce the Leash

Once your puppy is used to the collar, it's time to introduce him to the leash. Select a lightweight leash so there is no unnecessary pulling that may make your puppy leery of the leash. Clip the leash onto the collar and call your puppy to you. Some puppies will have a major reaction to the leash and thrash around wildly trying to get it off. This is normal, so simply drop the leash and allow your puppy to pull it behind him as he wriggles, squirms and hops. Do not let your puppy out of your sight since the leash can become caught up on something and hurt him. Continue to put the leash on for short periods of time, dropping down to one knee and calling your puppy to you with a reward when he comes. Once he reaches you, pick up the leash and walk him short distances around the house. Repeat this a couple of times a day until your puppy is accustomed to the leash. Make the process fun by verbally praising your puppy and offering treats. If he tries to bite leash, remember to tell him "No." Never let your puppy treat his leash like a toy.

After your puppy understands the sit and stay commands, you can teach him the "walk" command. You can do this with or without the clicker. Walk to your puppy, and say "walk" while you start walking. You should give him a treat if he walks in the same direction as you. You then ask him to sit and then stay, and remember to praise good behavior. You'll need to repeat this process until he starts to associate the word "walk" with the movement you're making.

Never pull or tug harshly on the leash, fight your puppy on the leash or yell at your puppy as those negative behaviors will only confuse the puppy and set your training back. Be patient with your pup and keep a consistent routine of attaching the leash and letting your pup get used to it slowly and at his own pace.

**His First Walk**

By now, your puppy is used to walking short distances inside the house on a leash and it's time to take the fun outside. The outside world offers a lot of fun and distraction, so even though your pup knows how to be led on the leash, he may act differently outside.

Go to the door and when your puppy follows, you'll need to tell him to sit and stay. Then you're going to put the harness or collar and leash on, finally opening the door. If the puppy reaches the end of his leash, then tell him to sit and stay. If he shows improper behavior due to excitement, just ignore it. Give him a treat when he follows the commands.

If he pulls, stop, stand completely still, and do not move until he comes back to you. If he is becoming too much to handle, always try the sit and stay command instead of pulling or shortening the leash he's on. Let your dog smell things, use the bathroom, have fun, and walk around the space with you. Be patient. Start with short walks at first and soon you and your pup can increase the time and distance.

Just make sure that you stay in the leadership role, and then repeat the process with different rewards. He'll start to eventually associate his collar or harness as well as the leash with walking with you, which will make him excited. You can start to add new commands as you test new boundaries with your puppy. For example, if you put the leash on the left, then you can teach him to turn left.

If you have it on the right, then he can learn to turn right. When it's just straight above him, then your puppy will know to keep walking straight. If you want to teach your dog to eventually walk without a leash, you can start by teaching him hand signals. When he starts listening to how to walk, then he is ready for trails, dog parks and other new places.

## If He Sees Another Dog

Your dog is bound to get excited with his new adventures. If your puppy sees another dog, he is likely to want to rush up to them. He might want to do this if he sees another person too, which means he could forget the commands that you taught him. You'll have to remind him that he listens to you by tightening or shortening the leash a little. This will pull your puppy right towards you, which will limit his ability to pull away or jump.

Tell your puppy to sit and repeat the command, and then tell him to stay. Reward him if he exhibits proper behavior. It can take several tries to get them to calm down, but this is essential to training a puppy properly.

This is why it's important to have treats with you when you take your puppy on walks. Most of the time, telling him he's good and petting him is enough, but sometimes a treat is needed or just wanted. Food is one of your most powerful motivators, but make sure that you change where you keep the treats on you. You don't want your puppy to just start listening because he sees you going for a treat.

**The Length of Walks**

You may be wondering how long your puppy should be on his walk, and this is based on different factors. Keep in mind how warm it is, how much stamina he has, and how long you want to go on a walk. If the temperature is too hot or too cold, then you won't want to take your dog on a long walk. If it's too hot, make sure that you keep a lot of water on you. A dehydrated puppy can get sick.

Puppies have different stamina based on their breeds. If they have fat bodies or shot legs, then they're not going to be able to walk as long or as far. If you have a bigger breed that's known for their endurance, then an hour's walk may be right up their alley. You should read up on your dog breed to know how long your walks should be.

Distance is up to you since you're the leader, but don't forget to keep his stamina as the weather in mind.

## Crossing Roads

You don't want your puppy to be so excited that he crosses the road without you and gets hurt by accident. This is one reason you taught him to sit and stay. It's important to ask him to sit and stay at a cross road before giving him the walk command. This is important even if your puppy is on a leash. Puppies do sometimes get off leashes, and it will decrease the chance of him getting hurt by a car if he knows to sit and wait at a crossing. This process is slow, especially with how excited he is when he's out, so make sure that you're willing to put in the time and effort.

# Chapter 9    Tricks, Tips, Exercises To Train Your Puppy

The most common age for people to train their dogs is the puppy stage. This is also known to be the hardest stage because their attention span is short, and they are easily distracted. To have the best possible training experience, you will want to work with these factors and not try to force your dog to change what is natural for them at their age.

## Know Your Puppy Before Training Begins

Before you bring your puppy home, start to do a little research. Get to know the main parts of your dog's personality by reading about their breed. All dog breeds tend to have their own characteristics, but your dog will also have their own personality. For example, your dog's breed might be on the shy side, but you notice your dog tends to warm up to people quickly. You then learn that not every dog from this breed is the same. In fact, most dogs remain hesitant around people they do not know.

Once you get your new family member home, spend time with them. You want to play with them, talk to them, and observe their behavior. Dogs need time to play and be by themselves and this is the perfect time to watch your dog's behavior. You also want to observe your dog's behavior when you are playing with them and when they are eating.

While you want to know the house rules before you bring your puppy home, if you want them to become comfortable quickly you will not become critical of them immediately. You won't harshly discipline them. Instead, you will understand that your puppy is learning their new environment and focus on giving them affection. You won't allow them to run wild in your home, but you will need to be patient when enforcing the rules.

When your dog is comfortable, they are going to listen to you better. They will follow your rules and the relationship between you and your dog will continue to grow strong. If you focus on rules before affection, your relationship will suffer. They will become more fearful of you, which can cause them anxiety. This will make training harder for both you and your dog. To correct your dog, keep your voice soft and start using simple words, such as "no." Always remember when your dog listens you should praise them with positive reinforcement.

Within a couple of weeks, you will have a good handle on your puppy's behavior. Expect their behavior to change as they grow, because it will. They will grow naturally as they age, with training, and becoming comfortable with their living environment. Once you feel your dog is comfortable and you should start to understand some of your dog's body language, which will help you understand your dog throughout the training process. For example, you will realize when your dog needs a break and when something is wrong.

The best time to start training a puppy is when they are a few months old. Professional trainers often say the best time to start training your puppy is between twelve to sixteen weeks old as this is known as the "golden period" (Klinger, 2019). This is the time when your dog will understand praise means they did something well, making them more likely to repeat the behavior.

One of the reasons it is important to get to know your puppy before training begins is that it allows them to get to know you. They will also understand certain pieces of their environment, making training a little easier over time. Once you feel your dog is comfortable in their new home with you and are old enough, you can start training your puppy with the basic foundations, such as home base, potty training, sitting, and going to bed.

**Tips for Training Your Puppy**
Puppies are quick to learn, but they can also cause a lot of stress in training. The key is to remember a few tips to make you and your dog's training experience the best.

## Have Patience

Even though your dog is a quick learner, you will still need to practice patience. Puppies become distracted easily, they have trouble concentrating because of their short attention span, and they tend to be stubborn from time to time. This means that if your puppy doesn't want to focus on training, they are going to find something else to focus on.

You need to keep in mind that a lot of this is biological for your puppy. It takes time for them to learn how to read your behaviors and understand what you want from them. Don't become angry if your dog keeps becoming distracted during training. If this is frustrating, take a bit of a break and try again later. If you seem to have trouble gaining your dog's attention every time you are trying to start a training session, enroll them in an obedience school or talk to a professional trainer for advice.

## Your Puppy Is at the In-Between Stage

Your puppy is not an adult or an infant. There are in-between stages when it comes to dogs. They are still developing mentally, physically, and emotionally and this can cause stress with training. At the same time, puppies can fool you. Because they are young, you may think they can't do a lot of tasks but think again. Puppies can do a lot more for themselves then they let on.

This age can also be tough for trainers because they struggle to know what their dog can handle and what it can't. The key to remember is that you need to take training one level at the time. Teach your dog the basics first, such as sitting, getting down, not jumping, laying down, and home base.

Train them on one trick at the time because they will become overwhelmed trying to learn more than one at once. Once they have a good hold on one trick, spend a couple weeks practicing this trick in your home and out in public. When they listen to you with very few mistakes, start training them on the next trick. Always remember to continue practicing the previous trick.

## Your Puppy Has Fears

No matter how long you spend focusing on giving your puppy a comfortable home when they first come into your front door, they are going to be afraid. They may show you their fear and they may not. Some dogs try to hide their fear because they have a need to prove they are "fearless." Don't become concerned if your dog shows fear immediately. They are unsure of their new environment, you, and your other family members. They will need time to warm up.

During the puppy stage, they are going to act startled from time to time. This happens when they meet someone new or they hear a strange noise. You may see them jump, look around, sniff, and then continue on with their task. This is normal behavior for a puppy. When your dog doesn't seem to calm down and continues to show signs of fear is when you need to consider taking them out of the environment. Signs of fear include:

- Not eating or eating very little
- Not drinking water like they usually do
- Looking around the room
- Trembling

- Whining
- Trying to escape the area to avoid what is frightening them
- Diarrhea
- Unable to control their bowel movement
- Vomiting
- Panting excessively
- Salivating

If your puppy starts showing these signs and not letting up, it is time to take them out of the environment. Spend some time alone with your dog to comfort them and let them know that it is okay. Don't force them to go back into the environment if they don't have to. Chances are they will continue to feel afraid because something is causing them to feel this way.

If your dog is over five weeks old and continues to show these signs, they may have inherited fearful tendencies from one of their parents. In this case, you will need to talk to your dog's veterinarian or a professional trainer who can help you ease your dog's fears. This is important because your dog will remain fearful for the rest of their life if their fearful tendencies as a puppy are not taken care of.

## Understand Your Puppy's Developmental Stages

In general, there are five developmental stages for puppies. Unless you have your dog from when they are born, you will not see all of the puppy's developmental stages. Once the puppy reaches their fifth stage, they are considered an adolescent dog.

## Stage One: Neonatal Stage

Stage one occurs within the first two weeks after the puppy's birth. This is a crucial time for a puppy and their mother to bond. During this stage, it is essential that you check on the mother and her puppies to ensure they are healthy, and all puppies are eating, but don't focus on spending too much time with the puppies.

This is time for the mother and if the mother feels people are spending too much time with her puppies, she will become uneasy and want to move them somewhere else. The mother is the strongest influence for the puppy. They will begin to taste and touch right after they are born.

## Stage Two: Transitional Stage

This stage starts when the puppy is two weeks old and goes until they are four weeks old. The puppy's behavior is heavily influenced by their mother. Therefore, you don't want to cause any stress on the mother. Even dogs feel overwhelmed by their new litter and are prone to aggression and depression easier. If your puppy feels this from their mother, they are more likely to show these characteristics later.

During this stage, the puppy will start to hear and smell. Their eyes will open, and they will start to stand, walk, bark, and wag their tail. At first, this won't happen a lot, but you will start to notice an increase in movement and sound coming from their location. Near the end of this stage, the puppy will see well, and they will start to show their teeth.

## Stage Three: Socialization Stage

At this stage, puppies start to have longer stages of development. The socialization stage will start before the puppy is fully out of the second stage and it will last until they are twelve weeks old. During this stage, you want to make sure your puppy is getting all their social needs met, even if you don't bring them home until near the end of this stage.

There are several milestones during this stage:

1. Play time becomes important between three to five weeks old.

2. Puppies become more aware of their surroundings, people, and animals around them, and their relationships.

3. Puppies are highly influenced by their littermates between four and six weeks old. It is during this time they start to act more like a dog.

4. Starting at five weeks old, you need to make sure your puppy gets a lot of human interaction but start slowly. You don't want to overwhelm your puppy in the beginning

because they will be a bit frightened by every new person they meet. Try to ensure all the interactions with humans are positive as this time sets the tone for how the dog is going to react to humans throughout their life.

5. Curiosity increases and puppies start to get into everything. It's always a good idea to "puppy proof" your home. They will also need more supervision during this time period so they don't get into anything that can harm them.

6. The puppy's senses are fully developed starting at seven weeks. However, they will continue to work on their coordination ability. This is always a fun time to watch your puppy as they start to stumble and see what their small body is capable of.

However, watch to make sure they don't hurt themselves as they will try to go up and down the steps and jump onto any piece of furniture. If they see other pets or their mom doing something, they will want to try too!

7. Around week eight is when you want to start house training your puppy. The first step should be potty training.

   Week eight is when your puppy will start to show true fear and the signs previously discussed. Spend a lot of time comforting your puppy when they become afraid.

8. Week nine is a great time to start training your puppy how to act around people. You always want to start small. They should understand the word "no" by this point. If they don't, it's a perfect time to incorporate this word into your training.

9. If they don't respond to their name, start the training process so they know to come to you when you call. It will help ease you and your puppy into more training in the next phase.

## Stage Four: Ranking Stage

This stage starts at about month three and goes to six months. This is when the puppy starts to understand ranking, such as dominance and submission. Because of this, you want to start training your puppy and establish the owner-dog relationship. The more they understand that you are the one who gives them orders, the easier training will go throughout their life.

During this stage, you want to make sure your puppy has time to play with other dogs. Allow them to play with dogs of any breed and size. As long as they won't hurt your puppy, they will start to thrive in understanding the ranking system.

One of the biggest challenges during this stage is chewing. In general, puppies chew on everything because they are teething. Just like teething bothers babies, it bothers puppies. Unfortunately, there is very little people can do to help ease any teething pain. At the same time, you don't want them chewing on everything. Because they take part in the action so often, it's best to train them not to chew on unwanted items at this stage.

One way to keep a puppy from chewing on something they shouldn't is to distract them. This works because puppies are easily distracted. While some people state this doesn't directly teach them not to chew, it is important to realize this is a temporary stage for a puppy.

You also need to be very careful when training your dog not to chew because there are items they can chew on, such as a dog treat, bone, toy, etc. Some people will give their dog a chewing toy when they catch them chewing on a pillow. Over time your puppy will understand they are to chew on their toys and not the pillow. Remember to give them positive reinforcement every time they start chewing on their toy over another item.

You can also take the object they are not supposed to chew on away and say "no." You don't need to sound harsh when you say no, just directly stating the word lets your puppy know that they shouldn't chew on that item. The key is you need to be consistent. Another tip for chewing is to play more with your puppy. When dogs are tired, they tend to stay out of mischief.

## Stage Five: Into Adolescence

The adolescent stage starts at about six months and lasts until eighteen months of age. There are more challenges with this stage than the previous stages because dogs tend to challenge people more during this time.

# Chapter 10    Dog Treating

How many times have you heard a friend or family member tell you about some crazy food that their dog loves? Dogs do love a massive variety of foods; unfortunately, not all of the foods that they think they want to eat are good or great for them. Dog treating is not rocket science but does take a little research, common sense, and paying attention to how your dog reacts after wolfing down a treat.

I am going to throw out some treats for training as well as some regular ole "Good Dog" treats for your sidekick and friend in mischief. I will touch on the proper time to treat, giving the treat, types, and bribery vs. reward.

Giving the Treat

Try to avoid treating your dog when he is over stimulated and running amuck and in an unfocused state of mind. This can be a counterproductive treating as it may reinforce a negative behavior or you may be unable to get your dog's attention.

When giving the treat allow your dog to get a big ole doggie whiff of that tasty food treat, but keep it up and away from a quick snatch and grab. Due to their keen sense of smell, they will know long before you figure it out that there is a tasty snack nearby. Issue your command and wait for him to obey before issuing the doggie reward. Remember when dog treating to be patient and loving, but do not give the treat until he obeys. Try to use the treating to reward the kickback mellow dog not the out of control or over-excited dog.

Some dogs have a natural gentleness to them and always take from your hand gently, other dogs need some guidance regarding taking the treat from your hand in a manner that is gentle. If your dog is a bit rough on the ole treat grabbing hand, go ahead and train the command "Gentle" when giving treats. Be firm that from this point forth no treats will be given unless taken gently. Being steadfast with this decision will work well and soon your pup or dog will comply if he wants his tasty treat.

Time to Treat

The best time to be issuing dog treats is in between his or her meals. If training always keep the tastiest treat in reserve in case you need to reel your dog's attention back to the training session. Too close to meal times all treats are less effective so keep that in mind when planning you training sessions. Obviously if your dog is full from mealtime he will be less likely to want a treat reward than if he is a bit hungry, therefore your training session is apt to be more difficult and far less effective.

What's in the Treats?

Take a gander at the treat ingredients and makes sure there are no chemicals, fillers, additives, colors and things that just seem unhealthy. Certain human foods that are tasty to us do not go down the doggie palette too well so take note. Almost all dogs love some type of raw meat and or slightly cooked meats. In tiny nibble sizes, they work great to get their attention where you want it focused.

Many people like to make homemade treats and that is fine, just keep to the rules we just mentioned and watch and read what you are adding while you are having fun in the kitchen.

Reward vs. Bribery Dog Treating

The other day a friend of mine mentioned bribery for action when he wanted his dog to shake his hand. I thought about it later and thought I would clarify. Bribery is offering the food in advance to get the dog to act out the command or behavior. Reward is giving your dog his favorite toy, food, love, affection after he has performed the behavior.

Example of bribery - you want your dog to come and you hold out in front of you a huge mound of steak in your hand before calling him. Reward would be giving your dog the steak after he obeyed the "Come" command and came to you.

Bribed dogs learn to comply with your wishes only when they see food, the rewarded dog realizes that he only gets his reward after performing the desired action. This is also good as other non-food items can more easily be introduced as rewards when dog treating.


Choosing a Veterinarian

Before you talk to any veterinarians, ask around for recommendations from your friends, family, animal shelter, humane society, neighbors, co-workers, or breeder. As a last resort, you can try the phone book.

Once you have a list of veterinarians to speak with, come up with some questions you want answered before making a decision on any one practitioner. Since most veterinarians are rushed (because of an overflow of clients) you may be better off, if you can afford it, to narrow down your list to 1-3 practitioners to arrange a preliminary checkup. During that meeting you can ask any questions you want while watching the doctor for how they handle and take care of any issues that do arise.

Some questions to ask:

• How many doctors do you have on staff? What animals do you provide care for?

• Do you have emergency hours? If not, who do you recommend in case of an emergency?

• May I have access to my dog's lab reports and notes from his file, if requested? What is the protocol, if any, for doing so?

•   If my dog is sick, are there arrangements that can be made for overnight care?

•   Do you support alternative or supportive medicine?

•   Does your clinic accept insurance or payment plans?

•   Do you have any pets, or dogs, of your own?

•   Armed with these questions and an eye for how your potential veterinarian handles your dog, you should be able to choose a practitioner easily.

# Chapter 11    Common    Behavior Problems

Once you are able to train your dog a few of the commands, you will find that the puppy is going to behave the way that you would like. They will listen to the commands that you give and will get along with the family. However, each puppy is going to have a different kind of personality and it is possible that they will still deal with some problems that you will need to take care of.

Some puppies are not going to have any of these tough dog problems, and some are going to have a few that you need to deal with. Learning what your puppy is going to do when others come around, and what behaviors you need to fix and fixing them as quickly as possible, can be the key to having a puppy behave the way that you want. Some of the most common tough dog problems that your puppy may show and the steps you can take to deal with them include:

## Jumping up on Other People

Do you find that your puppy likes to jump up on you and other people? For those who know what this is like, know that this is actually a behavior issue that should not be encouraged. Owners find that it can be hard to get dogs, no matter the age, to stop jumping up on them and some of the other people who are around them. Even if you don't feel like this is a big deal right now, think about how you are going to feel about the dog jumping on you or someone else when they are 100+ pounds? It is better to train your puppy to not jump on anyone from a young age. It is easier this way and ensures that they aren't going to be toppling other people over either.

First, we need to take a look at why the puppy is likely to jump on you or other people. For the most part, this is because they are excited. They see you or someone else come through the door and because they don't have the necessary self-control yet, and they want to jump up to show how excited they are to see you. Or, there may be times when the puppy is going to jump up because they see some item in your hand that they want, and they jump up to try and get it.

Either way, it is important to learn how to stop the puppy from jumping up on you and knocking you and others down. You need to remember to be consistent. You can't discourage the jumping one day and then be excited to see them another day and be fine with the jumping. Also, you can't have your cake and eat it too. You can't allow the dog to jump on you, and then train them not to jump on other people. This confuses the puppy and won't help you or them out at all. You have to decide that the jumping is a bad behavior, and then work to train them not to do it.

The good news here is that you are able to follow a simple process in order to get your puppy to listen to you and do what you would like. As with all of the unwanted behaviors that we are going to bring up in this chapter, you need to be strict about not allowing the puppy to jump on you ever. As you are going through the training process, and you see that the puppy is trying to jump on you, use the following steps to help prevent the behavior:

1. Tell the puppy, "OFF."
2. Turn your body around so that your puppy is looking directly at your back.

3. When you move the body so that it is turned around, the puppy is going to automatically get their paws back down on the floor and where they should be.

4. After the puppy has put their paws down, you can turn to face the puppy and then redirect them until they are sitting down.

5. Once the puppy listens and actually sits down, pet them, and reward them, showing the puppy that this is the way you want them to get your attention.

6. Now, there are going to be some times when the puppy will attempt to jump up on you again. If they start to do this, stop providing them with attention, and go through the steps above again. Only give the puppy some attention and affection when they are sitting down.

7. Practice with this each time that you come into the house, and even purposely leave for a few minutes so that you get some more practice. Over time, this is going to become a habit, and the puppy will learn that they are not supposed to jump on you.

The point of doing this is to show the puppy that they are only going to get attention when they sit, rather than getting any attention when they are up and moving and jumping on others. This will help stop them from jumping on you and can do some wonders for teaching them some self-control along the way.

## Destructive Chewing

Another issue that a lot of puppies will fall into is that they will start to chew on a lot of things that they shouldn't, many items that you do not allow, and are not part of their chew toys. When you first bring a puppy home, especially if they are only about eight weeks old, remember that they don't know what is and what is not allowed to chew on. You have to step up and teach them these rules. Sure it is easy to get frustrated with the puppy when they chew on the wrong thing, but you have to be proactive and teach your puppy what is appropriate behavior, especially when it comes to chewing.

While it may feel like the puppy is purposely being naughty and just had to go after your favorite pair of shews, remember that there are a lot of reasons why the puppy is chewing in the first place. They aren't trying to be naughty, and they aren't trying to make life more difficult for you. Some of the reasons that your puppy may be chewing on things include:

1. Dogs have a need that is instinctual that tells them to chew on things.
2. Chewing is a good outlet for most puppies when it is time to exert energy. Your dog could be chewing on a variety of items when they have a lot of energy that they need to get rid of, or when they feel a bit bored with their activities.
3. Similar to what we see with infants, puppies like to put objects into their mouths in the hopes of figuring out what the object is, and what they should do with it.
4. Puppies will often chew when they are teething. This chewing method is going to be a good way for them to soothe their gums.

Your dog is going to chew, and they need to chew, no matter if they are a brand new puppy or you have had them around for some time. You can't stop them from chewing, but you can control what they are allowed to do this with. You just need to pick out the right chew toys or items that you are going to give to the puppy and teach them what they can chew on, and what they need to avoid.

The good news is there are a few things that you are able to do in order to make sure the puppy is going to chew on the right items, and that they won't start to chew on some of your favorite items or on anything that they shouldn't have their mouths on. Some of the rules that you are able to follow when it comes to this include:

1. Always have some approved chewing objects that you can give to your puppy. Your puppy is going to chew no matter what, so make sure that you provide them with some toys or objects that they are allowed to chew on instead of getting mad when they chew on items that you don't approve of.

2. Be strict with what they can chew on, and what they can't chew on. In the beginning, you have to be strict on this and may have to keep the puppy confined to one area. But this is their learning period, and you are going to see the best results when you can keep track of the puppy and make sure that they don't get ahold of things they shouldn't have.

3. Redirect the puppy to an object that you approve of for them to chew on. The puppy is sometimes going to get away from you and will try to chew on something that they should not. When you catch them in the act, don't try to shout or yell or get mad about it. This just encourages them because the puppy sees that they are getting attention from this. Instead, when you find them, say "NO" and then redirect them over to an item that is designed for them to chew on.

**Pulling on the Leash**

Another common issue that you will see when you bring home a new puppy is that they like to pull on the leash. This one seems to be a really hard problem for most dog owners to deal with, and it seems like most owners are going to allow their puppy to pull on the leash forever. The good news is that it is possible to train your puppy to stop pulling on the leash, making things a whole lot easier for you.

The bottom line to remember here is that your leash should never be tight when you try to take the puppy on a walk. A loose leash is going to be the standard that you set, and it means that there is a little bit of slack on the leash between the puppy and you. There are a few reasons why you would want this to happen. It is going to teach the puppy that you are the pack leader and they should respect you. You don't want the puppy to start to think that they get to lead you all the time. When the puppy decides to make the leash tight and pulls on it, it is going to add a ton of stress and pressure to the neck, and this can be harmful to them. Pulling can also cause some damage to your own joints on the shoulders and arms. And when the puppy goes with a loose leash, it is going to become a much more enjoyable walk for both of you.

Now, this brings up the question of what you are supposed to do when the puppy decides to pull on the leash when you are walking. This may slow down your walk a bit, but you will find that most puppies are going to catch on quick, and doing this can really make a difference in how well the walk goes. Taking some time now will help you have much more pleasant walks overall. Some of the steps that you are able to do to help stop the puppy from pulling on the leash will include:

1. Any time that you feel the dog is getting excited and starts pulling on the leash, stop right where you are and don't go any further.

2. When the puppy starts to see that you have stopped and looks back at you, work with the clicker word.

3. Wait for the puppy to walk back to you, and when the puppy does this, reward them with a treat.

4. If you notice that the puppy is not coming back to you, lure them back using the heeling position and with a treat if you need it.

5. Now, there are some times when the puppy is still not going to come over to you. If this is the case, you can take another step back. Continue to do this until the puppy starts to walk back to you.

6. Repeat this process as many times as you need during the walk until the puppy learns that the leash needs to be loose.

As you can imagine, this is going to slow down the walk for a bit. You may only want to go on a walk down the block or so until the puppy starts to get the hang of what you are doing. The good news here is that the puppy will learn, and you will get the puppy to walk alongside you, with a nice loose leash rather than one that is tight and harming both you and the puppy, in no time.

**The Puppy Doesn't Want to Walk on the Leash**

There are some puppies who are so excited to go on a walk that they will bounce around, and then, once you are outside, they are going to pull on the leash, and you need to work on that problem. But then there are the puppies that don't like to walk on the leash at all. This is common for puppies who haven't been exposed to the leash at all. Most of the time they are going to catch on pretty quickly though, you just need to do a few steps in order to make this work for you. Some of the steps that you can use to get your puppy more used to the leash and doing what you want with it include:

1. Pull on the leash a bit, gently to the side while telling the command of "come" to the puppy.
2. If you find that this is not working, then call the puppy to you with a treat or something else that can be a reward.

3. If neither of the two steps above are working, you can try it with a harness and just repeat the steps that we have from above.

4. You will find that the harness can be a nice addition because it gives you a bit more control over the puppy while making it so that you don't put too much pressure on the neck of your puppy.

5. Once the puppy listens to you and walks over, reward the puppy with a treat and a clicker word.

6. If you find that the puppy is responding pretty well with this, try calling the puppy to you without the treat, and use the clicker word on its own as a reward.

7. Repeat the process again until your puppy gets more familiar with the leash and doesn't seem to mind it as much.

## Too Much Roughhousing with the Puppy

You will find that in some instances, your puppy is going to get into a really crazy mood where they will zoom around so much that they end up losing their self-control and won't behave well. When a puppy is in this kind of state, you will find that redirecting the puppy is not going to be enough. The more excitement that the puppy has, the harder it is to get the puppy to control themselves. This means that you need to step up and gain control before the puppy has their energy escalate too high.

This is going to require the whole family getting on board and making sure they are all on the same page. If the kids are working to rile the puppy up, it could get out of control before you even have a chance to slow it down a bit. The sooner you are able to slow the puppy down; the easier things are going to be for you.

What this means is if you see that the excitement of the puppy is starting to build, it is time to gain control right away. You can have them sit or do one of the other commands that gets them to stop and listen to you. Sitting is a good way to force the puppy to have some self-control and calm down.

Now, there may be some times when the puppy is going to be in this state already. This means that the puppy is going to have already lost their self-control, and you and the rest of the family may need to remove yourselves from the situation so that they don't exert this loss of control onto the kids or you at this time. Another option that can work with this is to put the dog in the leash and take them outside to wear out some of that energy or let them run in the backyard. This helps to get some of that pent up energy out, and then the puppy will be able to exert the self-control again.

## Fearfulness

There are some puppies who are going to be more reserved and may have some fears of the world, or at least a fear of things that are unfamiliar. It is natural to want to shelter them from the things that they fear, but this actually is going to cause the puppy more harm than good. The key in cases of fearfulness is to try and expose the puppy to the things that they are afraid of, but you should do it in a positive, as well as in a gradual, manner.

If you notice that you have a puppy that seems to be afraid of trying out anything new, or they have some fears that they can't seem to get over, there are a few steps that you can try out including:

1. Give your puppy some exposure to the thing that they are afraid of. Do this in a very slow manner so that they have time to look it over and explore it.

2. Start out with a big distance between the object the puppy is scared of and the puppy itself.

3. Associate the object of the puppy's fear with a lot of positivity. A good way to do this is to add something that the puppy really likes or really loves into that situation.

4. If your puppy is motivated by food, make sure that they are given a lot of treats while you expose them to that object.

5. Slowly start to move the puppy a bit closer to the object that they are scared about. Let them have some time to gain comfort with each distance to the object.

   1. Keep in mind that slowly is going to vary based on the puppy and how they are reacting to this process. You have to go at the speed and the distance that works the best for your puppy.

   2. If you find that the puppy seems pretty comfortable and unstressed, you may be able to approach the object of their fear on that same day. But for some puppies, moving them just a bit closer each day is going to be the best option.

You will need to repeat this process again and again, going a bit closer each day, until the puppy has been able to overcome their fears. Throughout the whole process, make sure to pay attention to the body language of the puppy, and learn their signals. You do not want to have them become too stressed out, and you don't want to push the puppy past their limits because this is just going to make things worse, and the puppy will start to fear the object more than before.

**The Escape Artist**

Hopefully you are able to read this part of the guidebook before the puppy has been able to escape out of your home and run away. Obviously, having the puppy escape and get lost is a traumatic experience for the whole family. But if the puppy is able to do this once, then it is likely they will continue to do this again and again.

There are several reasons why the puppy is going to try and get out of the home. They are allowed to roam freely, get into things, and do anything that they want. When they are out of the home, and away from you, they don't have to follow any of the rules any longer! Escaping is going to be a kind of self-rewarding behavior for a dog, and because of this fact, it is going to be a hard one to break if the puppy has already been able to do this.

This means that your goal needs to be to prevent the puppy from getting out and escaping from the home in the first place. Some of the steps that you can take to help prevent your dog from bolting or escaping from your home will include:

1. Make sure that you are fully aware of where your dog is each time that you are about to go out the door. Make sure that all of the people in the home, even visitors, are aware of this kind of rule.
2. Train your dog to sit and consistently wait before going outside can be useful for this, as well. It may take a bit more time and patience, and it is likely that the dog won't want to do it, but it helps them to know they have to sit still if they want to go out.
3. If your back yard has a fence, then you need to make sure that it is secure in every place. You do not want to have any places on the fence or

in the yard where your puppy will be able to get through.

4. If you do not have a fenced in back yard, then you need to make sure that the puppy is always on a leash.

The last point that is up above is going to be important. You may be tempted to keep the puppy off the leash because they have been behaving and have not been getting off the leash lately. But this gives the puppy a perfect chance to escape. You have to be consistent with this so that the puppy will know their boundaries.

## Too Much Whining and Barking

You will find that an excessive amount of barking is going to be a really frustrating behavioral issue that you, as a new owner of a puppy, will have to deal with. This is also one of the biggest stressors that come up with a dog and their owner. This is why it is so important to solve the problem before it gets to a level that is too hard to control.

First, you need to be able to understand why the puppy is barking so much in the first place. Some of the reasons why your puppy may be barking so much to start with will include:

1. To try and get your attention
2. Because they are uncertain or fearful about something.
3. They want to be able to assert their own dominance over a passerby or another animal.

There are different steps that you will need to take based on what the puppy is barking at. If you find that the puppy is barking at you at this time, then it is because they want to gain more control, or they want your attention. Whether your puppy wants to be with the rest of the pack or they need some more exercise or something else, this is a behavior that you need to correct right away. The steps that you can take to make this work include:

1. If you notice that the puppy continues to bark, turn your back to them and continue to ignore them until they stop.
2. Have some patience here because the puppy is going to continue their barking, in some cases, for a long period of time.
3. Once the puppy does stop barking, no matter how long it took, you can turn around and give the puppy lots of praise, treats, and attention.

4. Any time that the puppy starts to bark at you, repeat this process until they stop barking. This lets them know that you will only give them attention if they are not barking.

5. If you can't get the puppy to stop barking, then it is time to take a break in the crate until they are all done.

In some cases, the puppy is going to bark at passerby and animals. This issue is sometimes embarrassing when you bring your puppy in public, but some people may feel a bit frightened if they don't know your dog. Many times the owner is going to reinforce this behavior by screaming at the puppy to stop. You need to shift up the way that you respond to the barking first to get them to listen.

Let's say that the puppy is barking when they look at people or dogs through the window. Some of the steps that you are able to use in order to get the puppy to stop barking in this manner include:

1. Call the puppy's name in a positive manner so that they put their focus on you instead of the object of their attention outside.

2. The positive aspect of this is going to be the most important thing that you can do, but it is often the hardest as well. You need to find a way to be more motivating to the puppy than what they see outside.

3. Once the puppy does look over at you, reward them before refocusing their attention on something else that they like, such as a bone or a toy, so they don't get distracted again and start barking.

It is also possible that your puppy is going to start barking at some people and other animals when they are in public. You are not going to be able to demand that they listen to you in the same manner that you could when at home. But this also doesn't mean that you have to just let the puppy bark all day long while you are out in public, or that you have to go home. When you have a puppy who is barking at people and other animals when they are out in public, some of the steps that you can take include:

1. If you have a puppy who is already barking, it is time to move far enough away from the focus of their bark so that they stop the barking. If you are aware of a stimulus that may cause the puppy to bark, try to start out

far enough away so that they aren't going to bark at it to start with.

2. When the puppy is looking in the direction of the stimuli, call their name and do what it takes to redirect their focus back on you. When the puppy looks at you, give them a treat. This is going to help them to associate that stimulus with positivity.

3. As you get the puppy to self-control and calm down, see if you are able to move a bit closer to the stimuli. With each step, stop and redirect the puppy back to you, and get them to gain the self-control that you want.

   1. The degree you move is going to vary between each animal, so take your time and see what works for your dog.

4. During this process, make sure that you are the one who is maintaining the control, not the dog. Check on a regular basis that the puppy remains relaxed during this process.

5. If you move closer and your puppy starts to bark again, it is time to move further away and then work to focus their attention back onto you before trying again.

## Being on the Furniture

If you do not want the puppy to get up on your furniture, then this is another problem that you will need to work on as soon as possible. Remember that this one is up to you. Some people don't mind the puppy being on the furniture, and some don't want the puppy there at all. Either one is fine as long as you are consistent all the way.

For those who don't want their puppy on the furniture for one reason or another, this is just fine, but you need to start early, be firm with your decision, and be consistent. It isn't going to work if you sometimes allow the puppy on the furniture, and then other times, they are not allowed up there. It also will not work if you tell the puppy not to get on the furniture, but then others in the family allow the puppy to get up there.

If you have decided that you do not want to have your puppy to be up on the furniture, some of the steps that you are going to take in order to make sure that the puppy will stay off your furniture include:

1. Be strict right from the start and make sure that the puppy is never allowed on the furniture.

2. Any time that the puppy tries to jump up on the furniture, tell them "OFF."

3. Motivate the puppy to get off of your furniture and back to the floor by drawing them down with a treat or a toy.

   1. If you find that the puppy is not really willing to get off the furniture with this, then it is fine to guide the puppy down with the use of their collar to follow your No.

4. Make sure to reward the puppy with praise, a treat, and the clicker word when they do get off the furniture. Remember, with this one that prevention is going to be the best way to work through the behavior, and if you find that the puppy is heading for the couch, be ahead of the game and automatically direct them to sit and give them a reward in the process.

## Digging

While this is not really a behavior that is going to be bad for the puppy, it can be harmful to your yard, and this may be the reason that you stop it. Of course, most people don't want to look out in their yard and see a bunch of holes everywhere, so dealing with this problem right from the start can really help.

The first thing that we need to look at here is some of the reasons that a dog is going to dig. Each dog will be a bit different, but generally, a dog is going to dig because their breed has a genetic disposition to digging, they are using this to help them get their energy out, or they feel bored.

This is one of those times when it is best to be preventative to make sure the puppy does not dig. Exercising and stimulating your puppy can help them to not get bored, and it gets all of that extra energy out so that they are not likely to dig in your yard any longer. A puppy who is exerting all of their energy with playing with their toys, chewing on bones, and getting out on walks is going to find that they have no need to go to the yard and dig some holes. If genetics are the problem, then there probably isn't much that you can do preventatively with this one. You just need to learn how to correct the behavior to get it to stop with your puppy.

If you do happen to catch the dog digging in your yard and you want to get them to stop, there are a few steps that you are able to take. Some of these steps include:

1. If you find that your dog is already digging in your yard, tell them "NO" in a firm manner and get them away and distracted from the hole.
   1. If you can, immediately redirect him to an appropriate item he can exert his energy into, such as running around the yard or chewing on a bone.
2. If you find a new hole that you didn't catch your puppy digging, there is nothing that you should do about the behavior. You need to make sure that you catch them in the act. If it is after the fact, then you are out of luck.
   1. Remember that you are not able to discipline the puppy for something they did that you weren't able to catch them doing.
   2. Your puppy is not going to remember that they dug the hole, even if it was just a minute ago. Scolding the puppy later on, is not going to do you any good because the puppy won't have any idea what you are scolding them for.

As you can see, there are a lot of behaviors that your puppy may show off that are going to make life a bit harder when you are working with your puppy. It is best if you are able to be proactive with this process and learn how to deal with the behaviors before they get even worse. The sooner that you are able to deal with these problems, the easier it is going to be. Following the steps that are in this chapter will make it easier for you to really get your puppy to behave in the manner that you would like.

# Conclusion

Puppies can be very difficult to train if you are unsure of the proper steps. If you follow this simple step to train any puppy then your work will be easy. There is a lot of information within this book, and while you might feel a little overloaded, as many people do when they read a dog training book, you also feel more confident about training your new family member. Whether you brought home a puppy or an older dog, you have a great amount of information at your fingertips to help you and your dog through the training journey.

You can use this book to help your dog learn tricks from the puppy stage all the way to becoming an adult. At the same time, you can remind yourself of the common mistakes people make so you don't catch yourself doing the same thing. Remember, remaining mindful of your training, supervising your dog, and knowing where any of your training tools will help you stay consistent.

Use the tips and tricks that you see in this book wisely and make sure that you are able to understand them well and you will be able to have a very successful with training your puppy.

CPSIA information can be obtained
at www.ICGtesting.com
Printed in the USA
BVHW071157301020
592212BV00011B/707